CW00926653

Balancing Evils Judiciously

The Florida History and Culture Series

Balancing Evils Judiciously

The Proslavery Writings
of Zephaniah Kingsley

Edited and annotated by Daniel W. Stowell

Foreword by Eugene D. Genovese

University Press of Florida

Gainesville · Tallahassee · Tampa · Boca Raton
Pensacola · Orlando · Miami · Jacksonville

05   04   03   02   01   00   6   5   4   3   2   1

Library of Congress Cataloging-in-Publication Data
Kingsley, Z. (Zephaniah), 1765–1843.
Balancing evils judiciously: the proslavery writings of Zephaniah Kingsley / edited and
annotated by Daniel W. Stowell.
p. cm. — (The Florida history and culture series)
Includes bibliographical references and index.
ISBN 0-8130-1733-5 (cloth)   ISBN 0-8130-2117-0 (pbk)
1. Kingsley, Z. (Zephaniah), 1765–1843—Views on slavery. 2. Slavery—Florida—
Justification. 3. Slavery—Florida—History—19th century. 4. Florida—Politics and
government—1821–1865. 5. Florida—Race relations. 6. Social classes—Florida—History—
19th century. I. Stowell, Daniel. II. Title. III. Series.
E445.F6K56   2000
306.3'62'09759—dc21   99-28868

The University Press of Florida is the scholarly publishing agency for the State University
System of Florida, comprising Florida A&M University, Florida Atlantic University, Florida
International University, Florida State University, University of Central Florida, University
of Florida, University of North Florida, University of South Florida, and University of West
Florida.

University Press of Florida
15 Northwest 15th Street
Gainesville, FL 32611
http://www.upf.com

To Francis N. Stowell
Friend, example, Dad

CONTENTS

ILLUSTRATIONS

SERIES EDITORS' FOREWORD

Balancing Evils Judiciously: The Proslavery Writings of Zephaniah Kingsley is the tenth volume of a new series devoted to the study of "Florida History and Culture." During the past half century, the burgeoning population and increased national and international visibility of Florida have sparked a great deal of popular interest in the state's past, present, and future. As the favorite destination of countless tourists and as the new home for millions of retirees and other migrants, modern Florida has become a demographic, political, and cultural bellwether. But, unfortunately, the quantity and quality of the literature on Florida's distinctive heritage and character have not kept pace with the Sunshine State's enhanced status. In an effort to remedy this situation—to provide an accesible and attractive format for the publication of Florida-related books—the University Press of Florida has established the Florida History and Culture series.

As coeditors of the series, we are committed to the creation of an eclectic but carefully crafted set of books that will provide the field of Florida studies with a new focus and that will encourage Florida researchers and writers to consider the broader implications and context of their work. The series will include standard academic monographs, works of synthesis, memoirs, and anthologies. And, while the series will feature books of historical interest, we encourage authors researching Florida's environment, politics, literature, and popular or material culture to submit their manuscripts for consideration for inclusion in the series. We want each book to retain a distinct "personality" and voice, but at the same time we hope to foster a sense of community and collaboration among Florida scholars.

In *Balancing Evils Judiciously*, historian and editor Daniel W. Stowell brings together a remarkable set of documents. Zephaniah Kingsley's extended ruminations on the institution of slavery are the product of one of nineteenth-century Florida's most unusual citizens. As a British-born Loyalist who became a Danish citizen and international slave trader, then later as a wealthy East Florida plantation owner who had children with several of his slaves, Kingsley (1765–1843) marched to his own drummer. His long and loving relationship with his wife, Anna, whom he purchased in Cuba in 1806, was a source of scandal and amazement in the slave society of antebellum Florida. But flouting racial and sexual taboos was only part of Kingsley's heterodoxy. He had strong and unorthodox opinions on the rights and responsibilities of slaveholders, and little of what transpired on his sprawling St. Johns River plantations followed social convention or propriety. As the master of a remote borderland empire, he was able to think and act independently—and, for the most part, to ignore the objections and recriminations of his fellow planters.

In his masterful introduction, Daniel W. Stowell summarizes and contextualizes Kingsley's life and thought, preparing readers for an eye-opening series of primary sources. Beginning with the 1811 legal document manumitting Anna and three slave children sired by Kingsley and ending with the last will and testament written just before his death in 1843, this series of documents, which includes all of Kingsley's known writings on slavery, allows us to gauge the evolution of his proslavery thought. Each document enhances our understanding of an enigmatic man, but the most extensive, and certainly the most revealing, part of the collection is *A Treatise on the Patriarchal, or Co-operative System of Society, As It Exists in Some Governments, And Colonies in America, and in the United States, Under the Name of Slavery,* first published in 1828. It is here, in Kingsley's *Treatise,* that we see the full measure of his attempt to reconcile the perceived dictates of race and class, patriarchy and economic gain, morality and personal privilege. Kingsley found his own, imperfect way through this morass of conflicting loyalties and contradictions—a way influenced by personal idiosyncrasies and the myths and realities of the Florida frontier.

Thanks to Daniel Stowell's editorial and archival skills, Kingsley's writings join the expanding universe of accessible sources on the history of slavery in Florida—sources that promise to alter our understanding of how race and human bondage shaped a multicultural borderland that evolved into a modern state. As Floridians and other Americans continue to grapple with the troubling legacies of racial prejudice, discrimination, and exploitation, the Kingsley saga merits attention, respect, and thoughtful reflection.

Raymond Arsenault and Gary R. Mormino,
series editors

FOREWORD

Eugene D. Genovese

In 1828, Zephaniah Kingsley (1765–1843), a wealthy planter and former slave trader, published an extraordinary booklet, *A Treatise on the Patriarchal, or Co-operative System of Society,* which Dr. Stowell identifies as "the first formal articulation of proslavery ideology by a Floridian after Florida became an American territory in 1821." The *Treatise* went through new editions in 1829, 1833, and 1834, with small but noteworthy changes that Dr. Stowell has painstakingly traced. Kingsley defended slavery "as a necessary state of control [of] which no condition of society can be perfectly free," but he called for sweeping reforms to guarantee slaves human rights and prepare them for freedom. Indeed, much of what he advocated became the informal platform of a growing group of southern ministers, jurists, and others, which culminated in a powerful movement during the Confederacy.

Kingsley went much further than even the later clerical and juridical reformers dared or wished to go. While he staunchly defended slavery, he ridiculed racism. To be sure, Kingsley did not stand alone in his resistance to prevalent racial theories. From David Ramsay at the beginning of the nineteenth century to Joel Poinsett in the 1850s, some prominent southerners scoffed at the notion of innate black inferiority. Critics could be found in the churches from the early days to secession, although their voices steadily grew fainter over time. Outside the churches, William Byrd, in his *History of the Dividing Line,* casually remarked that all races have equal talents and that superiority and inferiority result from differences in access to improvement. The learned George Tucker of the University of Virginia, perhaps America's most able political economist, a broadly gauged intellectual of parts, and author of a valuable biography of Jefferson, regarded the current racial theories as nonsense. Although Tucker loved Jefferson and rarely took issue with him, he berated him for his untenable speculations on race.

Among other critics of racist doctrines, Sam Houston insisted to Tocqueville that blacks as well as Indians were as intelligent as whites and that any differences grew out of differing educations. But unlike Kingsley, most of these men had little or no affection for the proslavery argument.

Here, as on so many matters, Kingsley went his own way. He forcefully asserted that no society could expect to sustain itself without a measure of slavery in some form, but he no less forcefully asserted that class, not race, provided the bedrock of social relations. Pursuing the logic of his argument, he concluded that all property holders, regardless of color, must stand together in defense of slavery. Kingsley knew whereof he spoke, for as an experienced and successful slave trader, he had direct knowledge of Africa and kept up contact when he took to planting. And, in calling for an end to racial discrimination, he invoked the culture and experience of Brazil, Spanish America, and the West Indies.

As a strong proslavery man, he argued that race was beside the point and that a liberal policy toward free blacks and coloreds would secure their support for the regime. Indeed, as he well knew, the racist white planters of Saint-Domingue had virtually committed suicide by refusing the support of the numerous and powerful free colored planters, who initially wished to stand with the whites in defense of slave property. The response to Kingsley's campaign for the fair and equal treatment of free blacks was, however, hardly encouraging. Florida proceeded to enforce a rigid two-caste system and to place free blacks under severe constraints. Kingsley praised the liberality of North Carolina, including its extension of the franchise to free blacks, as the proper way for the whole South to go, but by the mid-1830s even North Carolina had reversed its policy.

The peculiarities of Kingsley's thought placed him in a unique position in a debate that was moving to center stage in the South. During the 1850s, George Fitzhugh of Virginia and Henry Hughes of Mississippi published extraordinary treatises on "sociology," in which they proclaimed slavery—or "warranteeism," as Hughes preferred to call it—the normal and proper condition of all labor regardless of race and denounced the free-labor system as brutally exploitative and unjust to the laboring classes. The argument flowed irresistibly from widely held premises, although, as often happens, not everyone wanted to follow the logic to its conclusion. The argument ran: If, as we southerners believe, our slaves fare better than the workers in free societies, if slavery as a social system is proving more humane, stable and morally responsible than its free-labor rival, and if we are Christians who have the responsibility to offer elementary succor to our fellow human beings, then it surely follows that some form of slavery or personal servitude should be recognized as the Christian solution to "the social question." Kingsley, whose religious views remain obscure, wrote from a secular vantage point that nonetheless emerged as consistent with the views of the theologians.

By the 1840s this doctrine of "slavery in the abstract," as it came to be called, was rapidly spreading across the South, making especially heavy inroads among the theologians, preachers, and church leaders who largely controlled the educational system and whose influence among the common people as well as the elite would be hard to overestimate. The seeds of the doctrine lay in the widespread conviction that black slaves at home lived better and more securely than white workers and peasants abroad. The press, pulpit, and political stump steadily reported on the hard life of the world's laboring classes, most notably the factory workers and miners of Great Britain. The implication that, therefore, Christians who cared about the welfare of their laboring brothers in Christ should prefer slavery as a social system grew steadily, if slowly and often expressed in muted tones.

Kingsley had, however, taken a different tack, which made slavery a stage in the evolution of most if not all peoples. Scientifically, his view promised aid and comfort to the advocates of the doctrine of slavery in the abstract. Ideologically and politically, it threatened to embarrass them. For the doctrine of slavery in the abstract drastically reduced but also accommodated the racial argument. Put roughly, it asserted that the laborers of all races would benefit from some form of servitude but that the black race per se was especially fit for enslavement. Thus blacks provided a special case within a general theory. So far as I know, Kingsley did not respond directly to this challenge, but, given his own premises, he probably assumed that he had implicitly refuted it.

Kingsley's place in southern history and America's endless debate over race—to say nothing of his astonishing life—is only now beginning to be appreciated and explored. Thanks largely to Dr. Stowell and to Daniel L. Schafer, that exploration is now well under way. Dr. Stowell's opening essay constitutes a splendid biographical and analytical introduction to the man and his work, and his editorial work in presenting these fascinating documents places professional historians and the general public deep in his debt.

ACKNOWLEDGMENTS

When I began research in 1994 on the National Park Service's Timucuan Ecological and Historic Preserve, of which Zephaniah Kingsley's Fort George Island plantation is a part, I had no idea that I would uncover such rich historical material. While I was conducting the research for my 1996 study titled *Timucuan Ecological and Historic Preserve: Historic Resource Study,* Professor Eldon Turner of the University of Florida continually encouraged me to probe more deeply into Zephaniah Kingsley's curious antiracist, proslavery thought. Eldon has been a source of constant support and encouragement ever since.

Several other professors at the University of Florida have also contributed insights from their own areas of expertise, especially David Geggus, Jeffrey Needell, and Bertram Wyatt-Brown, for which I am truly grateful. Eugene Genovese and Larry Tise offered valuable comments on a conference paper drawn from this material.

I am also grateful to Daniel Schafer for sharing some of his prodigious knowledge of Kingsley's life and to Jeff Mosher for directing me to sources on Latin American history. Bruce Chappell of the P. K. Yonge Library of Florida History aided me with his unparalleled familiarity with the East Florida Papers, and Caleb Finegan, Doug Thompson, and María Teresa Holcomb provided expert translations of difficult early-nineteenth-century Spanish documents. Dane Hartgrove of the National Archives and Andy Moore of the University of Florida valiantly aided me with final long-distance research.

At the University Press of Florida, editor-in-chief Meredith Morris-Babb was enthusiastic about this project and helped to make it a reality. Gary Mormino, one of the editors for the Florida History and Culture series, offered me early encouragement in bringing Kingsley's writings into print. Outside readers Stanley Harrold and Douglas R. Egerton provided both gracious praise and valuable, expert suggestions for improving the manuscript. Thank you all.

Kathy Tilford, Brian Peters, and Roger Clark continue to amaze me with the energy and dedication that they bring to interpreting Kingsley's Plantation for thousands of knowledgeable, misinformed, or uninformed visitors each year. They are each a credit to the National Park Service and to the field of public history.

My colleagues at the Lincoln Legal Papers, especially Dennis E. Suttles, John A. Lupton, and Stacy Pratt McDermott, merit my appreciation for encouraging me even when they do not share my fascination with southern history. Thank you also to Cullom Davis, the director of the Lincoln Legal Papers, for encouraging all of my scholarship, not only that related to Abraham Lincoln's legal career. Thank you to Bill Beard, Marty Benner, Susan Krause, and Christopher Schnell for being patient colleagues, and to Carmen Morgan for being patient generally. Janet Noecker, Jane Ehrenhart, and Mary Ann Pohl of the Illinois State Historical Library deserve special appreciation for handling numerous interlibrary loan requests.

My parents, Francis and Eunice Stowell, and my brother, Timothy Stowell, have helped to shape my views of the present and the past. They imparted to me a love of learning and of history that have motivated me in many ways. The dedication of this volume is a small gesture of gratitude for my father's important influence on my life.

Miriam R. Stowell, my wife and best friend, patiently aided me in double-proofing each of the texts reproduced here, including all four editions of the *Treatise*. Her love and good humor toward my seemingly endless projects sustain me. She deserves much of the credit for the quality of this and all my work. My children—Samuel, Joseph, Rachel, and Benjamin—are my most precious treasure and my greatest legacy. Their love and laughter brighten my life.

EDITORIAL METHOD

The documents collected in this volume represent all of Zephaniah Kingsley's known writings on the subject of slavery and other documents that illuminate his peculiar proslavery views.[1] Only the "Manumission of Anna," the "Address to the Legislative Council of Florida," and the "Memorial to Congress" have survived in manuscript form, and only the latter two are in Kingsley's hand. Lydia Maria Child's letter regarding Kingsley and Kingsley's letters on Haiti appeared first in newspapers and only later in book or pamphlet form. Where possible, I have compared the two versions and noted differences. I have also carefully examined and compared the four editions of the *Treatise* and noted all differences except minor, obvious printer's errors.

This edition reproduces each of the texts retaining the original spelling and punctuation, when doing so does not interfere with clarity. However, I have silently corrected obvious printer's errors in published documents. I have retained Kingsley's erratic punctuation, capitalization, and spelling in the "Address to the Legislative Council" and the "Memorial to Congress" because these documents offer the only direct evidence of Kingsley's writing style without editorial changes. I have indicated interlineations with a caret (^) both before and after the interlinear text. Where additional punctuation or words are necessary for clarity, I have added them, enclosed in brackets. I have combined the texts of the four editions of Kingsley's *Treatise* into one

1. The single exception is a letter to the *East Florida Herald,* signed "Rationalis" and published in the December 26, 1826, issue of the paper. Because the language is a virtual repetition of paragraphs in the "Address to the Legislative Council of Florida," it is not included in this volume. Other Kingsley documents in addition to the "Manumission of Anna" exist in the East Florida Papers collection of documents from the Second Spanish Period (1783–1821) of Florida's history, but they do not illuminate his proslavery thought.

document with the changes among the editions noted as follows. Text in unbracketed type appeared in all four editions. Text within brackets differed from edition to edition. Superscript years before the closing bracket indicate the dates of the editions in which the bracketed text appeared— 1828, 1829, 1833, and 1834.

The best we can do in this world is to balance evils judiciously.

ZEPHANIAH KINGSLEY, JULY 1842

Introduction

Daniel W. Stowell

In 1828, Florida planter and slave owner Zephaniah Kingsley presented an intriguing defense of slavery titled *A Treatise on the Patriarchal, or Co-operative System of Society, As it Exists in Some Governments, And Colonies in America, and in the United States, Under the Name of Slavery, With its Necessity and Advantages.* What makes Kingsley's contribution to proslavery thought remarkable is that it effectively separated race and class or condition. While upholding the legitimacy, necessity, and utility of slavery, his *Treatise* simultaneously assaulted contemporary notions of complete black inferiority. Kingsley insisted that a three-caste social structure, in which free people of color formed a large middle caste between whites and the mass of enslaved blacks, was best suited to Florida's climate and economy. This system, common throughout the Caribbean and South America, had served the Spanish well in Florida. Laws recently passed by the American territory's Legislative Council, however, oppressed free blacks[1] and forced them to identify racially with slaves against the white ruling class.

1. In both the introduction and the documents that follow, the term *free blacks* refers to all free people of color. White southerners, including Kingsley, used the term to refer to all free people of color, including those with only a small minority of black ancestors. However, they also sometimes made more sophisticated distinctions among "Negroes," "mulattoes," and "quarteroons"/"quadroons." In the 1850 census, 75.4 percent of "Free Negroes" in Florida were categorized as "mulattoes" (mixed racial ancestry); in 1860, 69 percent of Florida's free Negro population were. In 1860 in the Lower South, an average of 75.8 percent of the free Negro population were of mixed ancestry, but the proportion in the Upper South was 35 percent. The distinction between the two free populations stems from different emancipation patterns. In the Lower South, slave owners like Kingsley often manumitted their mixed-race offspring, while in the Upper South, slave owners were more likely to free their entire enslaved work force. Robert Brent Toplin, "Between Black and White: Attitudes Toward Southern Mulattoes, 1830–1861," *Journal of Southern History* 45 (May 1979): 185–200; U.S. Department of Commerce, Bureau of the Census, *Negro Population, 1790–1915* (Washington, D.C.: Government Printing Office, 1918), 220–21; Russell Garvin, "The Free Negro in Florida before the Civil War," *Florida Historical Quarterly* 46 (July 1967): 8; John Boles, *Black Southerners, 1619–1869* (Lexington: University Press of Kentucky, 1984), 135.

Kingsley urged Floridians to make "a considerable sacrifice of local prejudice to the shrine of self interest" by upholding the traditional three-tiered
system and uniting free blacks and whites through common economic interests. Kingsley's *Treatise* was the first and most important formal articulation of a proslavery ideology by a Floridian after Florida became an American territory in 1821. It also clearly reflected Florida's distinctive history
among the southern states as having been a Spanish colony (only Louisiana
had a similar past). More importantly, Kingsley's separation of race and
class in the southern social order contrasted sharply with the thought of
most other southerners, who increasingly collapsed all distinctions between
free people of color and slaves.

Born in Bristol, England, in 1765, Zephaniah Kingsley, Jr., was the second child and oldest son of Zephaniah Kingsley, Sr., and Isabella Johnstone
Kingsley. In 1770, Zephaniah Kingsley, Sr., migrated with his wife and family of five small children to Charleston, South Carolina, where he became a
successful merchant. In the 1780s, Zephaniah Kingsley, Jr., returned to
London for his education. As Loyalists during the American Revolution,
Zephaniah Kingsley, Sr., and his family fled Charleston for Britain's still-
loyal colonies far to the north in 1784.

As a young man, Kingsley probably worked aboard trading ships and
became a merchant. By 1793 he was back in Charleston and had declared
his loyalty to the American government. Later in the 1790s, he spent some
time in Haiti, traveling over the island as a coffee buyer. In 1798, Kingsley
became a Danish citizen and continued his career in maritime commerce.
During this time, when "slave trading was very respectable business," he
bought and sold human beings in the transatlantic slave trade. In 1802, for
example, he sold a cargo of African slaves in Havana. Not only did he
purchase slaves in the Caribbean for importation into various slave colonies, he also made voyages to Africa in 1805 and 1806, where he traded in
the dangerous East African waters. In 1803, Kingsley once again changed
his citizenship when he declared his loyalty to the Spanish crown and became a citizen of the Spanish colony of East Florida.[2]

2. Daniel L. Schafer, *Anna Kingsley*, rev. and exp. ed. (St. Augustine, Fla.: St. Augustine
Historical Society, 1997), 10–11. On the transatlantic slave trade, see James A. Rawley, *The
Transatlantic Slave Trade: A History* (New York: Norton, 1981); Hugh Thomas, *The Slave
Trade: The Story of the Atlantic Slave Trade, 1440–1870* (New York: Simon and Schuster,
1997).

Kingsley's slave-trading activities and interracial family have spawned a considerable
amount of folklore, mostly false. For one of the most blatant examples of Kingsley mythology,
see Branch Cabell and A. J. Hanna, *The St. Johns: A Parade of Diversities* (New York: Farrar

When Kingsley arrived in Spanish East Florida, he petitioned Governor Enrique White for land based on the provisions of the Royal Order of 1790, which invited foreign settlers to come to East Florida. White refused to grant the land, and by November 1803 Kingsley grew tired of waiting. He purchased four contiguous plantations (2,600 acres) on the western side of the St. Johns River near present-day Jacksonville from Rebecca Pengree, the widow of William Pengree. Kingsley asked the governor's permission to bring ten slaves from South Carolina into East Florida to begin working his new plantation. Over the next four years, he imported at least fifty-four more slaves and acquired other slaves by purchase. By 1811, he owned approximately one hundred slaves, who labored on his four plantation complexes. His black work force tended approximately two hundred acres of cotton, one hundred and fifty acres of provisions, and seven hundred orange trees.[3]

He bought some newly arrived African slaves (*bozales*) in Havana, Cuba, in 1806. One of the teenaged slaves whom he purchased there, Anta Majigeen Njaay, became his wife. They were "married in a foreign land," where the ceremony was "celebrated and solemnized by her native African custom, altho' never celebrated according to the forms of Christian usage." Between 1807 and 1811, Anna Madgigine Jai (as he called her) bore him three children—George, Martha, and Mary. In the latter year, Kingsley manumitted Anna and their children. Zephaniah and Anna Kingsley had another child, John Maxwell Kingsley, in 1824.[4]

Kingsley also had children by others of his female slaves or former slaves. Kingsley had one child, Micanopy, by his slave Sarah Murphy. In 1828, he emancipated his twenty-year-old slave Flora Hanahan, and over the next decade she bore at least four of his children—Charles, James, William, and Osceola. He may also have had a child—Fatimah—by Munsilna McGundo.

and Rinehart, 1943), 160–71. Philip S. May raised some of the mythology about Kingsley to the status of scholarship in "Zephaniah Kingsley, Nonconformist (1765–1843)," *Florida Historical Quarterly* 23 (January 1945): 145–59.

For a more careful investigation of one incident from the folklore that arose around Kingsley's life and the historical circumstances behind it, see Jean B. Stephens, "Zephaniah Kingsley and the Recaptured Africans," *El Escribano: The St. Augustine Journal of History* 15 (1978): 71–76. For further investigation of this same incident and the fate of the African slaves, see Gail Swanson, *The Africans of the Slave Ship Guerrero* (Marathon, Fla.: privately printed, 1998).

3. Daniel W. Stowell, *Timucuan Ecological and Historic Preserve: Historic Resource Study* (Atlanta: National Park Service, Southeast Field Area, 1996), 40–41.

4. L. Maria Child, *Letters from New-York* (New York: Charles S. Francis, 1843), 144; Schafer, *Anna Kingsley*, 18–19.

All of his mulatto children were either born free or were emancipated with their mothers.[5]

The Patriot Rebellion (1812–14), an abortive attempt by English-speaking settlers in East Florida to wrest control of the colony from the Spanish and annex it to the United States, devastated Kingsley's agricultural operations. Seminole Indians attacked Kingsley's Laurel Grove plantation in July 1812, captured or killed forty-three of Kingsley's slaves, and burned all of the outbuildings. When fellow Florida planter John Fraser died in 1813, Kingsley served as coexecutor of his estate and replenished his labor force by purchasing 158 slaves from Fraser's estate in 1816.[6]

With the failure of the Patriot Rebellion, John Houstoun McIntosh, the leader of the Patriots, fled into exile in Georgia. During the rebellion, invaders had ransacked McIntosh's plantation on Fort George Island at the mouth of the St. Johns River. In the spring of 1814, McIntosh sold the island to Kingsley, and Zephaniah and Anna Kingsley, their three children, his slaves, and her slaves moved to Fort George Island. For the next two decades, Fort George Island would serve as Kingsley's primary plantation, while he developed his ideas about the interplay of race, class, and slavery.

5. Daniel L. Schafer, "'A Class of People Neither Freemen Nor Slaves': From Spanish to American Race Relations in Florida, 1821–1961," *Journal of Social History* 26 (spring 1993): 592–95, 604–5; Schafer, *Anna Kingsley*, 40–41, 45. For more information on Zephaniah Kingsley's life, see Daniel L. Schafer's forthcoming biography of Kingsley.

In 1823, Kingsley manumitted "my negro child Patty aged about Two years the daughter of Sophy Chidgigine." Whether Kingsley's phrase referred to paternity or simply ownership is unclear. Manumission, July 5, 1823, Manumission papers, St. Johns County Deed Book H, St. Johns County Courthouse, St. Augustine, Fla.

Kingsley's relationship with these women is complex at best. Daniel Schafer posits that Anna was the first wife and that the others were co-wives in a polygamous relationship similar to African patterns. However, Zephaniah Kingsley referred to only Anna as "my wife." He referred to Flora and Sarah as Flora Kingsley and Sarah Kingsley, but former slaves frequently took their master's surname, so the surname is inconclusive evidence of marital status. It also appears that Anna and Zephaniah Kingsley's marriage was never legally recognized. If it had been, she likely would have been unable to own property in land and slaves in her own name. Under American common law, married women transferred all property rights to their husbands while married. Kingsley's probate records contain no references to the dower rights due to widows.

How to refer to these women is also problematic. *Co-wife* implies a polygamous relationship that may not have existed, and *mistress* implies a degree of freedom of choice that these women of color did not possess. Perhaps *concubine*, without its specific Jewish religious connotations, better fits the mothers of Kingsley's children, other than Anna Kingsley.

6. *East Florida Claims: Case of Zephaniah Kingsley* (n.p., n.d.), 1–4; Adjudication, January 24, 1816, Escrituras, Bundle 380, East Florida Papers, Library of Congress (microfilm copy at P. K. Yonge Library of Florida History, University of Florida, Gainesville, Fla.). On the Patriot Rebellion, see Rembert W. Patrick, *Florida Fiasco: Rampant Rebels on the Georgia-Florida Border, 1810–1815* (Athens: University of Georgia Press, 1954).

Kingsley's slaves on Fort George Island raised primarily Sea Island cotton and provisions. Kingsley may also have grown oranges on the island as he had done at his Laurel Grove plantation. The slaves lived in a complex of thirty-two tabby slave cabins arranged in a semicircular arc south of the main plantation house on the northwestern tip of the island. Kingsley encouraged the formation of families among his slaves, and they lived in the cabins in family units. By 1830, Kingsley had more than two hundred slaves on his plantations in Duval County and in neighboring Nassau County to the north.[7]

In 1821, Spain relinquished its troublesome ownership of East and West Florida, and the two colonies became one American territory. Kingsley, a subject of the Spanish crown for nearly two decades, became a citizen of a territory of the United States. In mid-April 1822, President James Monroe appointed William P. Duval the territorial governor of Florida. Duval, in turn, recommended Kingsley and seven other men from East Florida to the president to serve on the Legislative Council of the new territory; however, Monroe did not include Kingsley among his appointees for the 1822 session. In February 1823, Florida's delegate to Congress, Joseph Marion Hernandez, recommended thirteen men including Kingsley as "fit and worthy persons to fill the Legislative Council of that territory, for the ensuing Session." On March 3, 1823, President Monroe, "reposing special Trust and Confidence in the Integrity and Abilities" of the men nominated by Hernandez, appointed them to serve as the Legislative Council for the coming year.[8]

The Legislative Council assembled in St. Augustine late in the spring of 1823. On June 2, the council appointed Zephaniah Kingsley, William H. Simmons, and Edward R. Gibson to a committee "to consider the duties of masters of slaves and the duties of slaves and free persons of colour, and the regulations necessary for their government; with leave to report by bill or otherwise." The council also referred a "petition from the free people of

7. Stowell, *Timucuan Ecological and Historic Preserve*, 42, 70–74; Duval County, Florida, Nassau County, Florida, Fifth Census of the United States, 1830. The walls of the cabins were constructed of tabby, a building material made of roughly equal parts of oyster shell, lime, sand, and water. Twenty-eight of the cabins measured 20 feet by 13 feet, and most had two rooms. Four cabins, at each end and in the center of the arc, were larger (25' by 19') and, according to oral tradition, served as the homes of black slave drivers.

8. Clarence Edwin Carter, ed., *The Territorial Papers of the United States*, vol. 22, *The Territory of Florida, 1821–1824* (Washington, D.C.: Government Printing Office, 1956), 406–7, 422–23, 616, 640–41. Two of the men originally nominated by Hernandez declined, but at least one of their positions was filled by a candidate that he recommended. See ibid., 629, 640 n.

colour" to a committee consisting of Kingsley, Simmons, and Peter Mitchell.[9] On June 19, Kingsley, "from the committee relating to coloured persons and slaves, reported that said committee could not agree and asked to be discharged, which was agreed to." On the same day, Gibson gave notice that he would bring a bill "concerning Slaves and free persons of colour" before the Legislative Council.[10] It is unlikely that Kingsley's resignation from the committee converted his fellow legislators, but neither the surviving proceedings nor the published acts of the Legislative Council indicate that a bill on Florida's black population was passed in 1823.

In 1824 the Legislative Council, with Kingsley no longer a member, passed "An Act Concerning Slaves," which governed the activities of Florida's slave population.[11] This legislation repealed and superseded "An Act for the Punishment of Slaves, for Violations of the Penal Laws of this Territory," passed by the Legislative Council at its first session in 1822. Under the new legislation, slaves were prohibited from assembling without an overseer present, striking or otherwise "assaulting" a white person, buying or selling "anything of value," keeping firearms, or traveling without a written pass. Owners could be fined for leaving slaves on their plantations without white oversight, for "cruelly" beating their slaves, or for employing slaves in work on Sunday ("except such as is of absolute necessity"). The 1822 act governing slaves had allowed justices of the peace to jail any "emancipated slave" who traveled out of his or her county of residence, without a copy of "the instrument of his or her emancipation." The 1824 act made no such provision and did not address the status or activity of free blacks at all.[12]

In early December 1826, Kingsley penned an "Address to the Legislative Council of Florida on the Subject of Its Colored Population," which was published in the St. Augustine newspaper. The impetus for Kingsley's essay

9. *East Florida Herald* (St. Augustine), June 7, 1823; *Floridian* (Pensacola), July 12, 1823.
10. *East Florida Herald,* June 21, 1823.
11. Only two men from the twelve-member 1823 Legislative Council—Peter Mitchell and William Reynolds—were reappointed to serve on the 1824 Legislative Council. William Graham Davis, "The Florida Legislative Council, 1822–1838" (M.A. thesis, Florida State University, 1970), 152.
12. *Acts of the Legislative Council of the Territory of Florida. Passed at Their First Session 1822* (Pensacola, Fla.: Floridian Press, 1823), 181–85; *Acts of the Legislative Council of the Territory of Florida, Passed at Their Third Session, 1824* (Tallahassee, Fla.: Florida Intelligencer, 1825), 289–92; Thelma Bates, "The Legal Status of the Negro in Florida," *Florida Historical Quarterly* 6 (January 1928): 159–72; Julia Floyd Smith, *Slavery and Plantation Growth in Antebellum Florida, 1821–1860* (Gainesville: University of Florida Press, 1973), 101.

may have been his knowledge that the Legislative Council, meeting in Tallahassee, was prepared to pass legislation prohibiting the immigration of free blacks into Florida. Kingsley wrote, "Happily, perhaps for this Territory, little has been done as yet by Legislative provisions, of a permanent character, to influence the condition of the colored population either for good, or for evil." On December 30, 1826, however, the Legislative Council passed "An Act to Prevent the Future Migration of Free Negroes or Mulattoes to this Territory." According to the provisions of this legislation, no free blacks could enter Florida after March 1, 1827; any who did so would be fined $500. If unable to pay, they could be sold for one year to the highest bidder to pay the fine. Kingsley's "Address" served as an early articulation of several of the ideas that he would present two years later in his *Treatise:* the necessity for black labor in Florida, the advantages of a three-tiered caste organization of society, the importance of an alliance between free blacks and whites based on self-interest, the difficulties of inciting slave rebellion, the security of slave property, and the importance of laws to the stability of the slavery system.[13]

Not until 1828 did the Legislative Council pass laws specifically governing the free black population already living within Florida. In that year the assembly passed "An Act relating to Crimes and Misdemeanors committed by Slaves, free Negroes, and Mulattoes." This more comprehensive law consisted of sixty-three sections, which defined who would be deemed a slave, and enumerated a series of criminal offenses and their corresponding penalties for both slaves and free blacks. Free blacks could not possess firearms without a license from a justice of the peace or sell liquor to slaves. The Legislative Council reenacted the prohibition against free black immigration first passed in 1826. Even more ominously, several of the sections referred to actions by "any negro or mulatto, bond or free." These clauses collapsed all distinctions between free blacks or mulattoes and enslaved

---

13. *Acts of the Legislative Council of the Territory of Florida, Passed at Their 5th Session, 1826-7* (Tallahassee, Fla.: A. S. Thruston, 1827), 81–84; "Rationalis" [Zephaniah Kingsley], "For the Herald," *East Florida Herald,* December 12, 1826; "Rationalis," "To the Legislative Council of the Floridas," *East Florida Herald,* December 26, 1826; Z. Kingsley, "Address to the Legislative Council of Florida on the Subject of its Colored Population," c. 1827, manuscript in State Library of Florida, Tallahassee, Fla.

The Act passed by a 12 to 1 majority. Only Peter Mitchell voted against it. Born in Scotland, Mitchell was a successful planter on the upper St. Johns River. He served on the 1823 Council with Kingsley and again in 1824. In the first elected Legislative Council, voters chose Mitchell to represent St. Johns County and St. Augustine, the area most influenced by Spanish patterns of race relations. "Legislative Proceedings," *Pensacola Gazette and West Florida Advertiser,* March 30, 1827; Graham Davis, "The Florida Legislative Council," 52.

blacks or mulattoes. Prohibited activity under these provisions included "abusive or provoking language" toward whites, false testimony, administering "any poison or medicine whatever" with intent to kill, or "any other crimes or misdemeanors against the laws of this Territory." Slaves and free blacks would be punished in the same manner for the violation of these laws; forms of punishment included whipping and nailing the offender's ears to a post.[14]

Alarmed by the harsh restrictions on free blacks, as well as the collapse of many of the distinctions between free blacks and slaves, Zephaniah Kingsley again took up his pen to proclaim his vision of "the patriarchal society." Drawing on the ideas first expressed in his "Address to the Legislative Council" two years earlier, Kingsley expanded his condemnation of laws "dictated in a spirit of intolerant prejudice and irresponsible autocracy" in the first edition of his *Treatise,* published in 1828. Motives of self-interest, Kingsley insisted, dictated that through just laws white southerners should encourage free blacks to identify their interests with those of Florida's white population rather than with those of the slaves. Kingsley had good reason to assume that free blacks would unite with whites to quell slave unrest. Just such an alliance of free people of color with whites against slaves existed under French and Spanish rule in Louisiana, and these patterns continued when Louisiana became an American territory. Prosperous free blacks also held such an intermediate position in several cities across the South. It was George Pencil, a free black man, who exposed fellow free black Denmark Vesey's insurrection plot in Charleston, South Carolina. Pencil was more representative of the attitudes of free people of color than was Vesey himself, or, as Ira Berlin has concluded, "there were many more George Pencils than Denmark Veseys" in the antebellum South.[15] Laws such as those passed by the Legislative Council in 1828, Kingsley lamented, had the reverse effect of uniting free blacks with the enslaved black population.

Kingsley rightly noted that Spanish and Portuguese colonies in America had a more fluid racial and social hierarchy. Although whites remained at

14. *Acts of the Legislative Council of the Territory of Florida, Passed at Their Seventh Session 1828* (Tallahassee, Fla.: William Wilson, 1829), 174–90; John P. Duval, *Compilation of the Public Acts of the Legislative Council of the Territory of Florida Passed Prior to 1840* (Tallahassee, Fla.: S. S. Sibley, 1839), 216–28; Joseph Conan Thompson, "Toward a More Humane Oppression: Florida's Slave Codes, 1821–1861," *Florida Historical Quarterly* 71 (January 1993): 328.

15. Kimberly S. Hanger, *Bounded Lives, Bounded Places: Free Black Society in Colonial New Orleans, 1769–1803* (Durham, N.C.: Duke University Press, 1997); Ira Berlin, *Slaves Without Masters: The Free Negro in the Antebellum South* (New York: Pantheon, 1974), 270–73, 280–81; Boles, *Black Southerners,* 133–38.

the top and enslaved blacks at the bottom of their societies, free people of color could gain acceptance in free society and move to a higher social status through economic success. Racial barriers were more sharply defined in British, French, and Dutch colonies, but even those societies placed free people of color in the middle tier of a three-caste system that provided them with substantial privileges. In contrast, the United States developed a rigid, dichotomous system that elevated whites and oppressed all people of color, both free and slave.[16]

Kingsley's advocacy of uniting the interests of free people of color with those of whites mirrored the ideas of some planters within other slave societies in the Caribbean. In 1803, for example, Barbados Privy Council member John Beckles opposed a bill curtailing the ability of free people of color to acquire property. Recognizing the growing power of this small minority (2.5 percent of the population), Beckles argued,

> It will be politic to allow them to possess property; it will keep them at a greater distance from the slaves, and will keep up that jealousy which seems naturally to exist between the free coloured people and the slaves; it will tend to our security, for should the slaves at any time attempt to revolt, the free coloured persons for their own safety and the security of their property, must join the whites and resist them: but if we are to reduce the free coloured people to a level with the slaves, they must unite with them and will take every occasion of promoting and encouraging a revolt.

In 1830, a "Jamaican Proprietor" reflected a similar concern when he wrote to a Jamaican newspaper that whites should offset the numerical majority of free blacks by favoring the "free browns." White Jamaicans should "place the browns gradually on a footing with ourselves, to create a defensive alliance which may prove a security to us in our hour of need."[17]

Kingsley reiterated his call for the repeal of repressive laws against free blacks and their incorporation into a three-caste society in the second edition of the *Treatise* in 1829. Kingsley made only two substantive changes

16. Laura Foner, "The Free People of Color in Louisiana and St. Domingue: A Comparative Portrait of Two Three-Caste Slave Societies," *Journal of Social History* 3 (summer 1970): 406–30; Herbert S. Klein, *African Slavery in Latin America and the Caribbean* (New York: Oxford University Press, 1986), 217–41.

17. "Minutes of the Barbados Privy Council, November 1, 1803," Barbados Department of Archives, Barbados, quoted in David W. Cohen and Jack P. Greene, eds., *Neither Slave Nor Free: The Freedman of African Descent in the Slave Societies of the New World* (Baltimore, Md.: Johns Hopkins University Press, 1972), 233; *Watchman and Jamaica Free Press*, May 22, 1830, quoted in ibid., 203.

between the first and second editions. In the final note, Kingsley omitted his most sarcastic passage on slave religion and substituted a discussion of Gullah Jack (Jack Pritchard), a lieutenant in Denmark Vesey's abortive slave rebellion, whom Kingsley had purchased in Africa. From the same note, Kingsley also removed a sentence and a phrase discussing the 1828 Florida law that permitted public whippings of free blacks convicted of using abusive language toward any white person. The purpose of these minor changes seems to have been to make the *Treatise* less offensive. These passages contributed little to the primary argument, and their deletion represented a softening of some of Kingsley's harshest rhetoric.

Despite the protests of Kingsley and others, the Legislative Council of Florida continued to restrict the freedoms and the influence of Florida's free black population. An 1829 statute forced slave owners to pay $200 for every slave manumitted, and the freed person had to leave the territory within thirty days. In 1831 the council prevented justices of the peace from granting licenses for free blacks to carry firearms. In its 1832 session, the Legislative Council provided for free blacks to be sold to satisfy judgments against them; when sold, they would be "taken and held as a slave or slaves, and in all respects liable to the same penalties and treatment," until the judgment was satisfied. Furthermore, all free blacks over the age of fifteen were required to pay a territorial tax of $5. The same session of the Legislative Council also tightened the prohibition against the immigration of free blacks into Florida and forbade free blacks from assembling for divine worship or any other purpose. Prohibitions on immigration and restrictions on manumission had the desired effect. In 1830, Florida had a population of 18,385 whites, 15,501 slaves, and 844 free blacks. Although the slave population quadrupled over the next three decades, the number of free blacks grew by only 10 percent. In 1830 free blacks accounted for 5.2 percent of Florida's black population; among Lower South states, only Louisiana had a higher proportion of free blacks. By 1860, however, free blacks constituted only 1.5 percent of the state's African-American population.[18]

18. *Acts of the Legislative Council of the Territory of Florida: Passed at Their Eighth Session, 1829* (Tallahassee, Fla.: Floridian and Advocate Office, 1829), 134–35; *Acts of the Legislative Council of the Territory of Florida, Passed at Their Ninth Session, 1831* (Tallahassee, Fla.: Gibson and Smith, 1831), 30; *Acts of the Legislative Council of the Territory of Florida, Passed at the 10th Session, 1832* (Tallahassee, Fla.: William Wilson, 1832), 32–33, 129, 143–45; Berlin, *Slaves Without Masters*, 136–37, 396–99; Garvin, "Free Negro in Florida," 1–17.

In 1834 the Legislative Council repealed the 1832 law allowing free blacks to be sold for judgments against them. In 1835, the repeal was repealed, and the original law was revived

The most troubling act for Kingsley personally was "An Act to Amend the Act entitled `An Act Concerning Marriage License'." This law, passed in 1832, made it illegal for "any white male person . . . to intermarry with any negro, mulatto, quarteroon, or other coloured female." White women were likewise not allowed to marry any "coloured male person." Marriages in violation of this statute were declared "utterly void and null," and offspring of such marriages "shall be regarded as bastard, or bastards, and incapable of having or receiving any estate real, personal, or mixed by inheritance." Clerks, justices, and ministers were forbidden to issue licenses for or to perform such marriages. White men who lived "in a state of adultery or fornication" with black women could be fined $1,000 and be disqualified from public duties, including serving on a jury or giving testimony in a case involving whites. In sum, such offenders would be treated the same as if they were black. Although Kingsley's family presumably had immunity because they had lived in Florida under Spanish rule, the new law brought into question Kingsley's ability to will his property to his children as he wished.[19]

Scholars have rightly noted the discrepancy between the letter of slave and free black codes and the reality of their enforcement, but the existence of proscriptive laws created a climate of uncertainty at best. His wealth and long residence in Florida undoubtedly shielded Kingsley and his family from the provisions of some of the laws, but the possibility of their enforcement led him to urge his heirs in his will to migrate "to some land of liberty and equal rights, where the conditions of society are governed by some law less absurd than that of color."[20]

In response to the laws passed by the Legislative Council in 1832, Zephaniah Kingsley became the author and the first of twelve signers of a memorial presented to the U.S. Congress early in 1833. The memorialists complained of certain laws passed by "the last Session of Council relating to free people of color." They were distressed by the law that levied additional taxes upon free blacks "because of their color" and allowed them "to be sold as slaves for life if they be too poor to pay these odious and unequal

---

with the provision that it did not apply "to any free negro, who was a resident in this Territory previous to its cession to the United States, and who has continued to reside in it to the present time." *Acts of the Legislative Council of the Territory of Florida, Passed at the Twelfth Session, 1834* (Tallahassee, Fla.: William Wilson, 1834), 35; *Acts of the Governor and Legislative Council of the Territory of Florida: Passed at the Thirteenth Session. 1835* (Tallahassee, Fla.: William Wilson, 1835), 315.

19. *Acts of the Legislative Council, 1832*, 4–5; Schafer, *Anna Kingsley*, 40.

20. Canter Brown, Jr., "Race Relations in Territorial Florida, 1821–1845," *Florida Historical Quarterly* 73 (January 1995): 290–92; Thompson, "Toward a More Humane Oppression," 333–34.

taxes." The dozen petitioners, many and perhaps all the fathers of free mulatto children, were especially outraged by the law that imposed a fine of $1,000 and the penalty of disfranchisement upon a white person who married "a coloured woman." Kingsley and the other memorialists appealed to the laws of Spain under which they had formerly lived. Under Spanish law, the mulatto children of white men and enslaved black women were free and "admitted to most of the rights of Spanish subjects especially to the natural and inherent right of legal protection from which they are now excluded." The petitioners asked that the customs and habits of Florida under Spanish rule be viewed "with great toleration and indulgence," so long as they were not "at War with the institutions" of the United States. The Legislative Acts of Florida, the memorialists insisted, "are now replete with many cruel and unjust laws but those of mental persecution and proscription for the virtuous and sacred ties of domestic life and parental affection are certainly the most tyranical and most repugnant to the free institutions of our republican government." Therefore, they requested that Congress repeal and annul "all those cruel, unnecessary and most impolitic laws not authorized by the Constitution of the United States."[21]

By the early 1830s, Kingsley was openly critical of Governor William P. Duval and began circulating a petition addressed to President Andrew Jackson, asking him not to reappoint Duval as the territorial governor. In response, Duval accused Florida's congressional delegate Joseph M. White of having authored the petition. White insisted in a letter to Secretary of State Martin Van Buren that Duval's accusation was false. "Mr. Kingsley," White continued, "is a classical scholar, who would consider it a degradation to be put on a footing with Governor Duval in point of intellect, or education." White also described Kingsley as "a respectable gentleman," who was only "exercising the right of a citizen" in petitioning the President to appoint some other person as territorial governor.[22]

---

21. Clarence Edwin Carter, ed., *The Territorial Papers of the United States*, vol. 24, *The Territory of Florida, 1828–1834* (Washington, D.C.: Government Printing Office, 1959), 800–802; Schafer, "'A Class of People Neither Freemen Nor Slaves,'" 594.

Kingsley may have held an idealized view of access to manumission in Spanish Florida. Jane Landers, in her study of blacks in St. Augustine, notes that "manumission was not a common practice in St. Augustine during the second Spanish period" and that "achieving freedom became more difficult in the last twenty years of Spanish rule in Florida," though it was still possible for a few slaves in St. Augustine to "move out of bondage and acquire the privileges that a free legal status entailed." Jane Landers, "Black Society in Spanish St. Augustine, 1784–1821" (Ph.D. diss., University of Florida, 1988), 161, 169.

22. Joseph M. White to the Secretary of State, March 10, 1831, in Carter, ed., *The Territorial Papers of the United States*, 24:508–13.

In 1833, Kingsley also issued the third edition of his *Treatise,* which had two important revisions. First, in light of laws against interracial marriage and miscegenation, Kingsley removed passages that praised the improved "shape, strength, and beauty" of the "intermediate grades of color." As in the second edition, Kingsley moderated his rhetoric in an attempt to gain a wider reading for his principal ideas. Second, Kingsley added a five-page appendix to the *Treatise* that addressed the reaction among southern state legislatures to Nat Turner's bloody rebellion in Virginia. In it, Kingsley reiterated his premise that the existence of a large class of free blacks, attached to whites by self-interest, would promote the stability and profitability of the slave system as a whole. He again appealed to the example of other slave societies in the Caribbean and South America, where, he argued, liberal manumission laws and the extension of many legal rights to free blacks promoted stability and order.

In 1834, Kingsley issued his fourth and final edition of the *Treatise.* Other than a few minor word changes, it remained much the same as the third with one exception. Kingsley had signed his name to the Preface in each of the first three editions; in the fourth, he signed it simply, "A Slave Holder." As the title page did not identify the author in any edition, the fourth edition was an anonymous publication. It remains unclear why Kingsley removed his name from the work after three editions.

Kingsley's proslavery thought shared certain elements with other southern defenders of slavery.[23] Early in the 1830s, Achille Murat (1801–47), a fellow Florida planter and an exiled nephew of Napoleon Bonaparte, characterized southern public opinion as believing "that slavery is necessary, but at the same time, frankly acknowledged to be *an evil.*" Murat countered this popular perception by characterizing slavery "in *certain periods of the history or existence of nations,* as a good." For example, like Kingsley, Murat believed that white men were unable to labor in the open fields of the southern climate. Therefore, black slave labor was essential in opening up and developing the new American territory into which Murat moved in 1824. Fifteen years later, Murat owned a plantation near Tallahassee, Florida, of more than 1,000 acres with a labor force of 108 slaves. Although his avowed

23. On the southern proslavery argument, see William Sumner Jenkins, *Pro-Slavery Thought in the Old South* (Chapel Hill: University of North Carolina Press, 1935); David Donald, "The Proslavery Argument Reconsidered," *Journal of Southern History* 37 (February 1971): 3–18; Drew Gilpin Faust, ed., *The Ideology of Slavery: Proslavery Thought in the Old South, 1830–1860* (Baton Rouge: Louisiana State University Press, 1981); Larry E. Tise, *Proslavery: A History of the Defense of Slavery in America, 1701–1840* (Athens: University of Georgia Press, 1987).

purpose "in writing on slavery, is by no means to defend it," Murat countered abolitionist arguments by insisting that slaves were better fed, better dressed, and had more security than white European laborers or peasants. Murat's idyllic description of plantation life echoes Kingsley's: "A well regulated plantation is truly a most interesting spectacle; all . . . is governed in the most perfect order." Each slave had a house, poultry, pigs, and a garden plot. Like Kingsley, Murat employed the task system of labor, in which slaves had considerable time for their own use. However, unlike Kingsley, Murat considered "free negroes and mulattoes" to be a "degraded race" and an "unfortunate but dangerous class."[24]

Like those southerners who viewed slavery as a necessary evil, Kingsley believed that "slavery is a necessary state of control from which no condition of society can be perfectly free." The purpose of such a state in Kingsley's thought, however, was not primarily racial but rather labor control. Although the northern states and other countries may not have had the institution of slavery, they did have similar forms of subordination and dependence, in Kingsley's view. Like southern proslavery writers who wanted to perpetuate slavery indefinitely, Kingsley insisted that when properly managed, "negroes are a safe, permanent, productive and growing property, and easily governed."

Kingsley also shared similarities in outlook with an older generation of proslavery writers who viewed the institution of slavery as an evil, necessary to maintain order in a biracial society. Such men as President Thomas Jefferson, Virginia jurist and law professor St. George Tucker, and Baltimore lawyer Robert Goodloe Harper owned slaves but were profoundly uneasy about the institution. To prevent the future race war they feared and to rid the United States of the black race, each of these men endorsed some form of gradual emancipation and colonization.[25]

Thomas Jefferson, whom Kingsley described as "the immortal Jefferson," suggested a plan of emancipation and colonization in his *Notes on the State of Virginia* as early as 1787. Ultimately, Jefferson hoped that all slaves and free blacks could be removed from the United States, but he did not offer a specific plan. In an 1824 letter to Jared Sparks, the editor of the *North American Review,* he explained he had not specified any "particular

24. Alfred Jackson Hanna, *A Prince in Their Midst: The Adventurous Life of Achille Murat on the American Frontier* (Norman, Okla.: University of Oklahoma Press, 1947), 216; Achille Murat, *America and the Americans,* trans. Henry J. Bradfield (New York: William H. Graham, 1849), 67, 73–74, 77, 80, 83. Bradfield's translation is of Murat's *Esquisse Morale et Politique des États-Unis de l'Amérique du Nord* (Paris: Crochard, 1832).

25. Jenkins, *Pro-Slavery Thought in the Old South,* 31, 53, 97–98.

Map 1. The Island of Hispaniola, composed of Haiti and the Dominican Republic. Spain settled the eastern portion of the island as early as the late fifteenth century and referred to it as Santo Domingo. In the seventeenth century, French planters settled the western third of the island and called their colony Saint Domingue. In 1697, Spain officially ceded the western portion of the island to the French and a century later (1795) ceded the eastern portion as well. From 1801 to 1809, the island was united under the government of Haitian leader Toussaint Louverture and his successors. In 1808–9, residents of Santo Domingo successfully revolted against Haitian rule and restored Spanish rule, but in 1822, President Jean Pierre Boyer of Haiti reunited the entire island under his government and the aboriginal name of Haiti. The residents of Santo Domingo revolted against Haitian rule again in 1844 and proclaimed the Dominican Republic.

place of asylum" in his *Notes on Virginia* because he thought "that in the revolutionary state of America, then commenced, events might open to us some one within practicable distance." "This has now happened," Jefferson happily declared. "St. Domingo has become independent, and with a population of that color only; and . . . their Chief offers to pay their passage, to receive them as free citizens, and to provide them with employment." According to Jefferson's calculations, with only a relatively small tax, "voluntary surrenders" on the part of slave owners, and fifty vessels "constantly employed in that short run," the United States could rid itself of its black population within twenty or twenty-five years.[26]

Kingsley's views on race and slavery also bore some resemblance to those of his contemporary Robert Goodloe Harper (1765–1825). Born in Vir-

26. Thomas Jefferson, *Notes on the State of Virginia* (London: Stockdale, 1787; reprint, Chapel Hill: University of North Carolina Press, 1954), 137–42; John P. Kaminski, ed., *A Necessary Evil? Slavery and the Debate Over the Constitution* (Madison, Wis.: Madison House, 1995), 266–67; John Chester Miller, *The Wolf by the Ears: Thomas Jefferson and Slavery* (New York: Free Press, 1977), 264–72.

ginia and reared in North Carolina, Harper was educated at Princeton and practiced law in Charleston, South Carolina, before serving in Congress from 1794 to 1801. After his congressional service, he moved to Baltimore, Maryland, where he established a successful law practice. Although a slaveholder, Harper, like Kingsley, rejected the notion of African Americans' inherent racial inferiority. However, also like Kingsley, he believed that slavery needed to exist for the stability and productivity of the social order. In contrast to Kingsley's prescription of a mediating and stabilizing role for free blacks, Harper thought that free blacks contributed to the instability of a slave society by arousing discontent among the slaves. Both came to believe that blacks could achieve their full potential only in a new political and social environment. By the early 1820s, Harper favored gradual emancipation and colonization as the solution to the problem of slavery in the United States. To that end, he actively supported the efforts of the American Colonization Society to establish a colony of freedpeople in Africa. Unlike both Jefferson and Harper, Kingsley only reluctantly supported colonization after it became clear that southern society would make no place for free blacks.[27]

In the 1820s, a younger generation of white southerners began to develop a more strident defense of perpetual slavery as essential to the peace and prosperity of the South. In doing so, they were reacting to such pressures as the controversy over the admission of Missouri as a slave state, Denmark Vesey's abortive rebellion in Charleston, South Carolina, the endeavors of the American Colonization Society, and the activities of abolitionist groups.[28]

By 1828, when Kingsley published the first edition of his *Treatise,* southerners continued to have a divided mind over slavery. Some still viewed slavery as a curse, which they inherited from previous generations but were powerless to end without initiating a race war. In 1828, while defending the South from northern attack in Congress, William Drayton declared, "Slavery, in the abstract, I condemn and abhor." However, other southerners defended perpetual slavery in militant terms. In 1829, for example, Governor Stephen D. Miller of South Carolina boldly declared to the state legislature: "*Slavery is not a national evil; on the contrary, it is a national benefit. . . . Upon this subject it does not become us to speak in a whisper, betray fear, or feign philanthropy.*" Other southerners joined him in frequent, sophisticated, and unapologetic defense of slavery. To the ex-

---

27. Eric Robert Papenfuse, *The Evils of Necessity: Robert Goodloe Harper and the Moral Dilemma of Slavery* (Philadelphia: American Philosophical Society, 1997).

28. Jenkins, *Pro-Slavery Thought in the Old South*, 65–81.

tent that proslavery writers were, as David Donald has contended, "hope-lessly nostalgic," defending an "idealized paternalistic society" that had once existed, Kingsley shared much of their tone. However, the object of his nostalgia was different; it was Spanish East Florida.[29]

Despite the similarities of elements of his thought with those of other proslavery theorists, Kingsley provided a unique proslavery perspective. Specifically, Kingsley diverged sharply from virtually all proslavery advo-cates by separating race and class in his analysis of "the peculiar institu-tion": "Few, I think, will deny that color and condition, if properly consid-ered, are two very separate qualities. . . . our legislators, for want of due consideration, have mistaken the shadow for the substance, and con-founded together two very different things." Kingsley emphatically rejected the common proslavery notion of inherent black inferiority. In doing so, he foreshadowed in some ways the views of "romantic racialists" of the 1840s and 1850s. These theorists insisted that there were differences between the races, but they viewed blacks as childlike, affectionate, docile, and naturally religious. Such characteristics, rather than rendering blacks inferior, made them the fit objects of particular paternal care. Proslavery paternalists like Kingsley, who considered "the slave as a member of his own family" and whose slaves, according to him, "love me like a father," used such ideas to ameliorate African-American life in slavery. More commonly, however, abolitionists developed the antislavery implications of romantic racialism and insisted that the institution of slavery took unfair advantage of African Americans' "innocence and good nature."[30]

Instead of viewing all African Americans as worthy only of perpetual servitude or forced emigration, Kingsley insisted that a free black middling class, endowed with legal protections and joined by self-interest to whites, was essential to the security and stability of a slaveholding society. He also differed with southerners who wanted to exert stricter control over slaves and free blacks. Kingsley advocated as essential to the safety of southern society the repeal of "tyrannical" laws and policies governing slaves and free blacks. It was these views and his mixed-race family that led his neigh-bors to call him an abolitionist by the early 1840s.

Unlike many proslavery theorists and later romantic racialists, Kingsley

29. *Register of Debates*, 20th Cong., 1st sess., 1:974–75; *Charleston Courier*, November 28, 1829 (italics in the original); Donald, "Proslavery Argument Reconsidered," 16. See William W. Freehling, *Prelude to Civil War: The Nullification Controversy in South Carolina, 1816–1836* (New York: Harper and Row, 1965), 49–86; Tise, *Proslavery*, 98–100.

30. George M. Fredrickson, *The Black Image in the White Mind: The Debate on Afro-American Character and Destiny, 1817–1914* (New York: Harper and Row, 1971), 101–2.

did not utilize Christianity as an element of his argument. Instead, he exposed what he viewed as the "danger and hurtful tendency of superstition (by some called religion)" among his slaves. Religion rendered slaves "unhappy and discontented with their condition in life." Kingsley's defense of slavery, therefore, was strictly secular and did not rely either on moral philosophy or scriptural argument. Likewise, his idea of "balancing evils judiciously," which so disturbed Lydia Maria Child and made him amoral in her eyes, was based on "rational policy" rather than on religious conviction.[31]

When it became apparent in the early 1830s that Florida and the southern states had decisively rejected his prescription of a three-tiered social order and had endangered the future prospects of his own mixed-race family, Kingsley reluctantly began to support colonization. Although he believed that slavery was necessary in multiracial societies in tropical and semitropical areas, Kingsley was willing to accept emancipation and colonization as a better alternative than the rigid system of racial slavery then consolidating in the United States, which left no place for his mixed-race family. In contrast, other supporters of colonization, like abolitionists Benjamin Lundy and Lydia Maria Child, viewed slavery as inherently evil. They endorsed colonization as a way to weaken through manumission and ultimately to destroy the institution of slavery in the United States. Lundy supported the colonization of freed slaves in Haiti in the 1820s. By the early 1830s Lundy turned his attention toward the Mexican province of Texas as a suitable site for black colonization. In his plans for Mexican colonization, two of Lundy's most active and important supporters were Lydia Maria Child and her husband, David Lee Child.[32]

In the fall of 1831, either Zephaniah Kingsley or his son George Kingsley wrote a letter to the *Working Man's Advocate* in New York, insisting that emigration had become necessary. The "imperious jaws of necessity and self preservation" forced free blacks in the United States "to free themselves from the state of bondage under which they now exist" without any "constitutional protection to person and property." The climate of Canada made it an unsuitable destination for free black emigrants. Instead, Mexico provided a "place of safety and permanent refuge." Although Mexico was at that time unstable politically, it was "conveniently situated," the people were "entirely free from all prejudice against complexion," and the consti-

---

31. For religious justifications of slavery, see Jenkins, *Pro-Slavery Thought in the Old South,* 200–241.

32. Merton L. Dillon, *Benjamin Lundy and the Struggle for Negro Freedom* (Urbana: University of Illinois Press, 1966), 87–102, 165–220; Deborah Pickman Clifford, *Crusader for Freedom: A Life of Lydia Maria Child* (Boston: Beacon, 1992), 121–25.

tution and laws of Mexico "recognize no difference of merit on account of color." However, the stability of the Mexican government did not improve in the early 1830s, and white American settlers continued to move into the province of Texas with their slaves, a migration that eventually led to war between the United States and Mexico.[33]

Four years after endorsing Mexico as a potential colonization site, Kingsley turned his attention to the island nation of Haiti. Although openly critical of African colonization schemes in the *Treatise,* he did argue that colonizers lost a "great opportunity" when they did not begin to settle freed slaves in Santo Domingo, the Spanish part of the island of Hispaniola, when the Haitians united the entire island under the Republic of Haiti in 1822. The Haitian government began in 1823 to redistribute land in sparsely settled Santo Domingo from the church and large landowners to freed-people and small farmers. Haitian President Jean Pierre Boyer also initiated a campaign to encourage black settlers to emigrate from the United States. Boyer advertised in American newspapers for prospective black emigrants, luring them with promises of transportation, free land, and Haitian citizenship. Although perhaps as many as thirteen thousand African Americans migrated to Haiti in the 1820s and 1830s, large numbers returned to the United States. Harsh conditions and the language barrier discouraged many, and in June 1825 the Haitian government suspended its practice of subsidizing immigrants' transportation expenses. Opposition to the land redistribution in the Spanish portion of the island forced the Haitian government to end this practice in 1826, but it continued to sell public lands to new settlers.[34]

By the mid-1830s Kingsley realized that his hopes for a three-caste society in Florida were lost, and he followed his own advice by inaugurating a personal colonization effort. In the autumn of 1835 he traveled to Haiti, "the Island of Liberty," where he made plans to establish an agricultural colony. In October 1836, Kingsley sent his son George and six male slaves, freed for the purpose, to what had been the Spanish portion of the island to begin the experiment. George Kingsley purchased land from the Haitian government on the northern coast near Puerto de Plata. A year later, Kingsley took his wife, Anna, and their adolescent son, John Maxwell Kingsley, to Haiti, along with George Kingsley's family and several slave

33. [Zephaniah or George Kingsley], "Prejudice Against Color," *Working Man's Advocate* (New York), October 1, 1831.

34. Alfred N. Hunt, *Haiti's Influence on Antebellum America: Slumbering Volcano in the Caribbean* (Baton Rouge: Louisiana State University Press, 1988), 165–73; Dillon, *Benjamin Lundy,* 87–103.

families, whom he also freed. Kingsley eventually moved his other mulatto children and their mothers to Haiti. Before he died, Kingsley had resettled at least fifty-three of his former slaves in Haiti. They remained there in a form of indentured servitude for nine years, after which they received land of their own. Other Kingsley slaves were not so fortunate; they remained in Florida, working his lands to finance the experimental colony in Haiti. "The best we can do in this world," Kingsley told the protesting abolitionist Lydia Maria Child, "is to balance evils judiciously."[35]

Kingsley encouraged others to emancipate their slaves and settle them in Haiti as well. To this end, he published *The Rural Code of Haiti, Literally Translated from a Publication by the Government Press, Together with Letters from that Country, Concerning its Present Condition, By a Southern Planter*. Although first published in 1837, the pamphlet was "put to press more than a year ago, but its publication was delayed by unforseen causes." By 1839, Kingsley had published two more editions of the pamphlet. The *Rural Code of Haiti* is a republication of a series of six laws passed in 1826 that governed various aspects of life in the Haitian countryside. Designed to enhance Haiti's faltering agricultural production, the rural code forced all agricultural workers to enter into labor contracts with landowners. The rural code provided detailed regulations to govern the duties of landowners and workers. It established a Rural Police to enforce its provisions and prescribed harsh penalties against vagrants and laborers who failed to work. Appended to the translation of the legislation was a series of four letters that Kingsley wrote from Haiti in 1835. The letters characterized the lush beauty and fertility of the island as well as its "pure republican" government, where color formed no barrier to advancement.[36]

The *Rural Code of Haiti* had been the subject of continual controversy since its promulgation in 1826, especially in the British press. American

35. Zephaniah Kingsley to the editor of the *Christian Statesman*, June 30, 1838, in [Zephaniah Kingsley], *The Rural Code of Haiti, Literally Translated from a Publication by the Government Press, Together with Letters from that Country, Concerning Its Present Condition, By a Southern Planter*, 2d ed. (n.p., [1838?]), 45–48; Schafer, *Anna Kingsley*, 41–44; Schafer, "'A Class of People Neither Freemen Nor Slaves,'" 594–95; Child, *Letters from New-York*, 145.

36. [Zephaniah Kingsley], *The Rural Code of Haiti, Literally Translated from a Publication by the Government Press, Together with Letters from that Country, Concerning Its Present Condition, By a Southern Planter* (Granville, Middletown, N.J.: George H. Evans, 1837; 2d ed., n. p., [1838?]; 3d ed., New York: J. Vale, 1839).

The first edition contained four letters written by Kingsley from Haiti in September, October, and November 1835. The second and third editions also included a fifth letter written by Kingsley from Washington, D.C., on June 30, 1838, to the editor of the *Christian Statesman*, which described George Kingsley's colony near Puerto de Plata.

proslavery theorists and even some British abolitionists insisted that the code proved that blacks would not work without the compulsion that the code provided. American proslavery writers praised the wisdom of Haiti's revolutionary leader Toussaint Louverture for initiating a stern forced-labor policy in 1800 to reestablish agricultural output. Haitian President Jean Pierre Boyer's decision to revive compulsory agricultural labor through the rural code only confirmed proslavery spokesmen in their belief that free blacks would not work unless forced to do so.[37] James Franklin, a British defender of the necessity of slavery, insisted that "it was evident to every man in Hayti, at all conversant with the negro character, that an attempt to keep up cultivation without force was impossible." "Left any longer to pursue their uncontrolled and unlimited propensity for indolence," Franklin argued, the Haitian people "must recede into barbarism and uncivilization." The rural code provided the solution because it "enforces labour with a rigid hand,—nothing more excessive can be demanded of the slave in the British colonies." Franklin even argued that "the slave is infinitely better off than the free labourer of Hayti."[38]

In contrast, abolitionist authors like W. W. Harvey insisted that the rural code "contains many judicious regulations with regard to agriculture." The necessity of those policies that "appear to infringe on the liberty of labouring classes" remained to be proved, but the code could never support the assertion that "the condition of those classes is again become, in all respects, similar to the condition of slaves."[39]

Zephaniah Kingsley died on September 13, 1843, while in New York City on a business trip. He was seventy-eight. Eighty-five of his slaves, valued at $30,000, remained in Florida to be divided among his heirs. Kingsley's will called for the distribution of his estate among his widow, Anna, their two sons, his sons by two other former slaves, and three of his white nephews. Other white relatives contested the will, citing the 1832 Florida statute that prevented the offspring of interracial relationships from

37. Hunt, *Haiti's Influence on Antebellum America*, 88–90.

38. James Franklin, *The Present State of Hayti, (Saint Domingo,) with Remarks on its Agriculture, Commerce, Laws, Religion, Finances, and Population* (London: John Murray, 1828; reprint, Westport, Conn.: Negro Universities Press, 1970), 334, 342, 367; David Geggus, "Haiti and the Abolitionists: Opinion, Propaganda and International Politics in Britain and France, 1804–1838," in David Richardson, ed., *Abolition and Its Aftermath: The Historical Context, 1790–1916* (London: Frank Cass, 1985), 134–36; Hunt, *Haiti's Influence on Antebellum America*, 132–34.

39. W. W. Harvey, *Sketches of Hayti; from the Expulsion of the French to the Death of Christophe* (London: L. B. Seeley and Son, 1827; reprint, Westport, Conn.: Negro Universities Press, 1970), xiii.

inheriting property from their white father. The Florida courts eventually upheld the will, and his black, white, and mulatto heirs received considerable amounts of money from his estate.[40]

Kingsley represented a small group of planters who had settled in Florida during the Second Spanish Period and who hoped to perpetuate the three-tier caste system of race relations under Spanish rule: whites, free blacks, and slaves. However, Florida became an American territory in the midst of what historian Larry Tise has labeled the "neglected period" of proslavery history. Between 1785 and the rise of radical abolitionism in the early 1830s, Americans reevaluated their revolutionary heritage and adopted a more militant and conservative proslavery ideology. Prominent among the publications marking the demise of America's flirtation with equalitarian ideals was Thomas Jefferson's own *Notes on the State of Virginia* (1787). During the 1820s and 1830s, Americans influenced by this ideology migrated to Florida, bringing with them a harsher, two-caste system of race relations: free whites and enslaved blacks. Successive legislative acts in Florida throughout the antebellum period, as in other southern states, reflected a sharpening of the distinctions between free and slave, white and black.[41]

By the time of Kingsley's death in 1843, Florida had firmly established a two-caste system of race relations. Free whites governed nearly the same number of enslaved blacks. A small group of free people of color remained, a dwindling reminder of Florida's Spanish past and of the contradictions between legal dictates and social reality. Their lives were increasingly proscribed, in law if not always in fact, and their freedoms were precarious. Unlike their counterparts in other slave societies, Florida's free blacks were never to become the large mediating and stabilizing force in the social hierarchy that Kingsley had envisioned.

40. Probate Record for Zephaniah Kingsley (1843), #1203, Probate Department, Duval County Courthouse, Jacksonville, Fla.; "Petition to Judge Farquhar Bethune from Martha McNeill et al.," October 1844, Kingsley Estate Papers, Item M87-020, File #1, Florida State Archives, Tallahassee, Fla.; May, "Zephaniah Kingsley, Nonconformist," 156; Schafer, *Anna Kingsley,* 45.

41. Tise, *Proslavery,* 41–42, 66–67, 347–48; Schafer, "'A Class of People Neither Freemen Nor Slaves,'" 589–609; Brown, "Race Relations in Territorial Florida," 287–307; Jane Landers, "Black Society in Spanish St. Augustine."

On immigration to Florida, see Edward E. Baptist, "The Migration of Planters to Antebellum Florida: Kinship and Power," *Journal of Southern History* 62 (August 1996): 527–54.

Manumission of Anna (1811)[1]

Liberty

In the name of Almighty God, Amen: Let it be known that I, D[on]. Zephaniah Kingsley, resident and citizen of the St. Johns River region of this province hereby state: That I have as my slave a black woman named Ana, about 18 years old,[2] who is the same [native African] woman that I purchased in Havana from a [slave] fleet which, with permission of that government, was introduced there; this Negress I have had and have procreated with to produce three mulatto children[3] named Jorge, three years and nine

1. Document Signed, Translation. Manumission, March 4, 1811, East Florida Papers, Reel 172, Bundle 378, pp. 21A–B, 22A, Library of Congress, Washington, D.C. (available on microfilm). Translation by Caleb Finegan, courtesy of Kingsley Plantation, National Park Service.

2. Anna Madgigine Jai (c. 1793–1870) was born in Senegal in Africa. Enslaved as a young girl, she was sold to Zephaniah Kingsley, Jr., in Havana, Cuba, in 1805. Sometime before 1828, she married Kingsley "according to her native custom," and they had four children together. She became a slave owner herself and managed Kingsley's plantations when he was away. In 1837 she emigrated to Haiti to escape the uncertainties of being free and black in Florida. After living in Haiti from 1837 to 1847, Anna Kingsley returned to Florida, where she lived for the remainder of her life near her two daughters. See Schafer, *Anna Kingsley*.

3. Kingsley first filed a manumission to free Anna and their three children on March 1, 1811, but Kingsley did not sign it, and the clerk wrote on the bottom of the document, "It did not pass." Three days later, Kingsley filed this document. The principal difference in the language of the two documents was that in the first, at this point in the text, Kingsley wrote, "this Negress I have had and have procreated with to produce three children whom I recognize as such, and because of my current status as a single man, illegitimate." In this second document, Kingsley dropped any reference to his marital status or to his children's legitimacy, though he continued to acknowledge his paternity. Thanks to María Teresa Holcomb, Lincoln Land Community College, Springfield, Ill., who aided me in discovering this distinction between the two legal documents.

months old;[4] Marta, twenty months old;[5] and Maria, one month old.[6] And focusing on the good qualities of the already mentioned Negress and for other causes, I have decided to give her freedom graciously and without any other interest, the same accorded to the aforementioned her three children. And so, to reduce all this to its simplest form, by this document, I grant that I free and liberate the aforementioned Negress Ana and the three children from their [conditions of] subjection, captivation, and servitude, and as a consequence I remove my rights of property, possession, utility, dominion, and all other royal and personal deeds, which [up to now] I have possessed over these four slaves. And I cede, renounce and transfer [my rights] to each of them so that from today forward, they can negotiate, sign contracts, buy, sell, appear legally in court, give depositions, testimonials, powers of attorney, codicils, and do any and all things which they can do as free people who are of free will without any burden.[7] Declaring them to be free of obligation (as I certify ^I the scribe^ according to that which comes from the book of mortgages in my possession which I reviewed) and obligating me to this statement and to the liberty which I give them through it, it will be certain and assured to them, and that I, and my heirs and successors will not contradict this in any way, and if it so happens that one of them should bring lawsuits or contradicting accounts, we desire that they not be heard nor admitted in a court of law since that which he attempts is not a right which pertains to him; and so it is observed that the approval and validation have been acquired, adding strength to strength and contract to contract, to which resolution I obligate myself with my present and future properties, power and submission to the justice of His Majesty in order that they compel me to its fulfillment as through a sentence granted and passed in authority of a judged affair about which I renounce all laws, privileges, rights, of my own volition, and in general in form which is prohibited. In whose testimony is dated in this city of St. Augustine, Florida, on the fourth of March, 1811. I, the scribe hereby give faith that I know the granter of these

4. George Kingsley (1807–46) married Anatoile Francois Vauntravers in 1831. He led his father's colonizing expedition to Haiti in October 1836. George Kingsley died when the ship on which he sailed for Florida sank during a storm. Probate Record for George Kingsley (1846), #1205, Probate Department, Duval County Courthouse, Jacksonville, Fla.

5. Martha Kingsley (1809–70) married a white New York native named Oran Baxter, a shipbuilder and planter. She lived in the Jacksonville area for the rest of her life. Schafer, *Anna Kingsley*, 41–42.

6. Mary Kingsley (1811–94) married a white New York native named John S. Sammis, a planter, sawmill owner, and merchant. She lived in the Jacksonville area for the rest of her life. Schafer, *Anna Kingsley*, 42.

7. Slaves in Spanish East Florida could legally perform none of these actions.

privileges and that I sign with witnesses Don Juan de Entralgo, Don Bartolome de Castro y Ferrer,[8] and Don Bernardo Jose Segui being present = [. . .] = I the scribe = it is valid.
Zeph. Kingsley
Attentively,
José de Zubizzareta
Scribe of the Governor[9]

8. Bartolome de Castro y Ferrer (b. c. 1759 in Spain) owned part of a plantation on San Pablo Creek. He owned fifty slaves in 1813. Biographical Files, St. Augustine Historical Society, St. Augustine, Fla.

9. Juan José de Estrada was the acting governor in early 1811, until Sebastian Kindelan y Oregon became the new governor in the summer of 1811.

Address to the Legislative Council of Florida (c. 1826)[1]

Address to the Legislative Council of Florida on the subject of its Colored population by Z. Kingsley, a Planter of that Territory

> Si genus humanum et mortalia temnitis arma at sperate Deos:/Virg.[2]
> Do nothing inconsistent with the Divine Law of self preservation. Modesty becomes criminal when not supported by firm Resolution.

No subject has ever excited more feeling or animosity of late years among all the sections of the U. States than that of the coloured Population. Proppositions & arguments how it would be best to dispose of it have been presented to the Public under so many different views that it seems hopeless to offer any new argument or to attempt to reconcile all the different feelings & interest upon this very interesting question. But violent and accrimonious feeling has got to such a Pitch that it seems necessary to do something for the preservation of our southern Property which must either rise or fall in value according as this subject is rashly or discreetly disposed of: Some indeed have been of opinion that this is too delicate a subject for public discussion[,] but I doubt very much the good foundation of any Pollicy that shrinks from rigid investigation in every shape[,] for how are we to correct evills without clearly understanding their causes? and liberty is but an empty name a mere burlesque if we fear to speak the truth. The writer of this is well a ware of the difficulty as well as danger he incurs by venturing to obtrude or declare his sentiments upon so delicate a subject and certainly would be deterred from touching it if he was not excited by a strong feeling of self Preservation which overcomes the fear of that danger. He being a Planter in florida whose only dependence for these last 20 years has been in

---

1. Autograph Document Signed. Z. Kingsley, "Address to the Legislative Council of Florida on the Subject of Its Colored Population," State Library of Florida, Tallahassee, Fla.

2. The quotation here is from Virgil, *The Aeneid*, bk. 1, lines 542–43. Translation: "If man thou scornest and all mortal power, forget not that the gods watch good and ill!"

the labor of his slaves, cannot in this case be suspected of any membership or community with manumating societies, nor does he pretend to any great talent or skill as a writer but having travelled in the earlier [years] of his life to Africa and even been concerned in the hideous traffic of slaves, and has either [been] domiciliated in or visited all the west India Collonies[,] where he spent several years also in Cuba and Saint Domingo as well as the main land of south america where both from motives of interest & curiosity he has paid minute attention to those numerous & mixed populations and to their government; moreover having lived originnally in the state of south Carolina he thinks himself competent at least to relate facts which may enable others to compare thes[e] facts and draw conclusions whereby we may Judge of the causes of results obtained by Legislative Acts in some cases so widely different from those obtained in others from the very same materials.

A certain portion or extent of country situated on the Seaboard of the southern states whose climate is unfavourable to the health and production of white people, seems destined by nature to be cultivated & brought into perfective value by the labor of coloured people; of all this portion of territory extending from the capes of Virginia so[u]therly to Cape Florida on the Atlantic coast and perhaps 100 miles back upon an average from the sea, Florida is by far the valuable. This does not arrise from any superiority in the extent or fertility of the soil, for it is perhaps naturally the l[e]ast favoured of the whole in this respect. Its intrinsic value is in the Climate which being warmed by a more vertical sun and containing considerable large bodies of very rich land brings sugar & other Tropical productions to a state of perfection unknown any where else within the United States of which government it has so ^lately become a member that men of Capital have hardly as^ yet had time to find it out or to appreciate those singular advantages which by slave or colored labor alone can be realised. Happily perhaps for this Territory little has been done as yet ^heretofore^ in the way of legislation either for the slave or free part of its coloured population of both of which it must necessarily be compounded and upon the discreet government of which its good or bad fortune must entirely depend. It lays now before the members of our Legislature like a gem untouched by the Lapidary[3] according to whose skill it either must become of incomparable value or ^an^ useless bauble. It therefore behoves those Gentlemen on whose skill so much depends to weigh & consider well the tendency of every movement so that on a subject of such infinite national importance no step

3. A lapidary is a cutter, polisher, or engraver of precious gemstones.

may be taken not warranted in all its bearings by well established Presidents [precedents] the salutary consequences of which have been tested both by known consequences and by comparative deductive reasoning. To arrive at which it will be necessary to consider the state of the various surrounding slave Collonies, to take a view of their Political establishment & regulations with their effects & consequences.

I believe it is generally admitted that our climate forms an insurmountable barrier to the cultivation of our soil by white People whose health sinks under the toils of agriculture in the Sun, for that reason we have no other alternative but either to abandon it or to employ colloured labourers which must consist of slaves as the class of Free People of colour is not yet suficiently numerous to be hired at reduced wages or such as comport with agricultural economy. This applies to People we are therefore to look for labour to that intrinsically valuable cast of People called Negro Slaves whose productive labour & cheerfull obedience has in all cases been measured by the Justice & good treatment of their master who is well renumerated for his kindness by rearing up a permanent & proffitable Estate: with which some of the least informed part of our Northern Neighbours have found great fault but of which I shall take no notice as all the economists who have considered the subject are sensible that it is a necessary condition in our Society and if that condition is comfortable & justly Dealt with perhaps it may bear comparison with the lowest agricultural conditions of countries or even may deserve a preference for although I beleave it to be a fact generally allowed the darkness of complexion measures the capacity for enduring heat and the suns Rays yet it is likewise admitted that very few People will labour to a greater extent than that to which their necessities oblige them or rather that their toils are measured by the comparative comfort they expect to derive from them: however to set all metaphysical queries at rest by Palpable facts, Our Population consists and to do well must consist of three classes or casts of people. First those called white or without mixture of African blood secondly free People of colour who are either black or sprung from coloured women & white men & lastly the most numerous valuable & Productive class the Slaves, mostly Black: Indians & other mixtures are too few to be noticed. In some of the colonies the coloured population bears a proportion to the white of ten to one or more and in others much less still instances of disturbance or revolt are rare: In two instances not very long ago viz: Barbadoes[4] & Demara[5] both were

4. See n. 32 on p. 67.
5. See n. 33 on p. 67.

traced to sources of delusion by Fanatical Preachers but were easily put down by the united force of the whites & free collored people whose interest were equally concerned in preserving peace and good order indeed it allways has been the uniform pollicy in all slave colonies to attach the Free people of valor [color] to the side of the whites so that both may be united and have one common Interest in keeping the slave Caste in subordination as their condition of not holding Property. However justly they may be other wise treated as slaves will in all cases require more or less constraint but moderation & justice which should be governing principals in every man entrusted with despotic power when added to the stronger influence the free people of Color naturally have over the slaves arrising from connection. Color common origin when added to good precept & example renders the slaves perfectly tractable & obedient and such is the entire confidence between all the casts that you will hardly find a hall door locked in the night on any of the foreign Plantations few of which have less than 500 slaves & I have known many instances especially among the Dutch Colonies where only one white individual resided on a large Plantation: I must observe that many of the Headmen & principal Drivers & mechanic are liberally treated and there is no law to hinder any slave having the means from geting his freedom.

It will naturally be asked what are the great temptations held out to the free Coloured population to induce them to place themselves on the side of the white? It is answered: Interest! Their person are secured from insult and their Property which they can hold in their own names of any kind or to any amount. They have Perfect & undisturbed enjoyment of all moral and municipal Rights except that of being eligible to Public offices. They are rich well educated Respected holding slaves & real Property and perform all the millitary & other duties of Yeomanry in other Countries. One law is peculiarly encouraging to them and exists either in law or fact generally viz. the white children of a free Quartroon are recognised as white by law.[6] It is but a few years say 1812 when about 50 colored militia inhabitants of this then Province saved by their Bravery and fidelity the City of St. Augustine from being taken & Plundered.[7] This one circumstance proves that they can be

6. See n. 9 on p. 46.
7. During the siege of St. Augustine as part of the Patriot Rebellion, a small detachment of free black militia effectively ended the siege. On September 12, 1812, a force of approximately fifty blacks and Seminoles under the command of Sergeant Prince Witten ambushed a group of approximately twenty United States Marines under the command of Captain John Williams in Twelve-Mile Swamp, north of St. Augustine. After the destruction or capture of the supply wagons that Williams's men escorted, Colonel Thomas Adam Smith and his men retreated

made very serviceable and surely if we have it in our Power to attach them to our Interest as friends it would be very impolite [impolitic] to make such Laws as would render them Enemies. In short I consider that our personal safety as well as the permanent condition of our Slave property is intimately connected with and depends much upon our good pollicy in making it the interest of our free colored population to be attached to good order and have a friendly feeling towards the white population. If we have no need of their help as soldiers, let them remain rather as friends in case of need for fear a day might come when they might be wanted by us or even induced to take part against us. It must make a very great odds in our peace of mind & personall security as well as in our physical strength as a community, whether by our pollicy we make it the Interest of a large & effective body of men to be our friends & firmly attached to us by the same interest and whom we are obliged to suffer to live among us; or by our want of Pollicy not only to detach and neutralize this body of people but to make these our decided Enemies by degrading them to the rank of our slaves & only waiting to pour down upon us a full measure of retribution for our injustice. For I believe it is allowed by all philosophers to be axiom in morality That every evill inflicted is exactly measured by a respondent quantity of resentment. The Laws of some older and more Powerful neighbouring states may be brought in opposition to this kind of Policy, but I believe that no beneficial effect or good tendency can be adduced as testimony of the wisdom of these laws & enactments which are in discreet [direct] opposition to civil liberty and the economy of self Preservation: as the conscious fear of revolt and the Military Government of those places abund[an]tly testify and precariously accomplish by fear of the Bayonet what might be naturally, permanently & pleasantly accomplished by the wise & unchangeable Laws of self preservation besides this: Pollicy that might be safe or merely tolerated in communities possessing a large Proportion of cool & healthy back country well calculated for the production of white People who are allways at hand ready

---

from St. Augustine, thus lifting the siege of the city. The Spanish government praised Witten and his men, declaring that it was "well satisfied with the noble and loyal spirit which animates all the individuals of this company." For their "good services to the country," some of the black militiamen received permission to appropriate weapons and provisions from the rebels' plantations, and three years later, several of them received land grants for their military service. J. H. Alexander, "The Ambush of Captain John Williams, U.S.M.C.: Failure of the East Florida Invasion, 1812–1813," *Florida Historical Quarterly* 56 (January 1978): 280–96; Jane G. Landers, "Acquisition and Loss on a Spanish Frontier: The Free Black Homesteaders of Florida, 1784–1821" in Jane G. Landers, ed., *Against the Odds: Free Blacks in the Slave Societies of the Americas* (London: Frank Cass, 1996), 93.

to put down any disturbance that might happen or to receive or protect the sea board inhabitants in case of war would in no way apply to our situation or correspond with our prosperity or even existence as an independent community: We have no back country or mountains to Shelter us we are nearly surrounded by the ocean, our being & prosperity must depend upon our own good Policy & wisdom in cultivating friendship with those populous, rich & powerfull Establishments which surround us every way. Nature by intersecting our Peninsula with rivers Lakes & innumerable water courses has destined us for a commercial as well as an agricultural people. Our Pollicy must be liberal and such as will meet the approbation of the U. States government & the world without which we never can rise to consequence or be happy in our independence.

The example of St. Domingo may be adduced as a circumstance in opposition to this Doctrine of liberal Pollicy to slaves & free colored people. But let it be remembered that the revolt of St. Domingo grew out of the French Revolution by a National Decree of Emancipation even that decree would have resisted the Revolutionary Storm but for the mischevous industry of Commissioners sent out on purpose to enforce the National Decree (Santhonax & Polvorel)[8] and this even would have failed to Revolt the slaves who were finally forced to take up arms by the inhabitants themselves by fighting one against the other. This blind violence of Party feeling is not peculiar to the French. The Inhabitants of St. Domingo were a liberal well educated generous people. We observe sparkling traces of the same spirit of Fanaticism every now & then bursting out among ourselves on that very subject. It is a humiliating proof of human weakness and should serve to warn us of the danger we incur by following our Passions instead of being guided by our reason & discretion. No stronger illustrations can be given of the difficulty of Revolutionising Slaves than was manifested in grand Anse[9] upon that very Island while that department was besieged by Generals Toussaint[10] & Rigaud[11] with two Powerful Armies of Blacks their own country men and preceded by all the ordinary inflamatory Proclamations of Freedom. This department was held at that time by the British who occupied the Town of Jeremie. The slaves continued faithfull on the Plantations where they worked and did their duty as usual during several years their Master besides their ordinary tools of agriculture had furnished the men with a Gun Bayonet & Ammunition to defend themselves. I heard of no

8. See n. 13 on p. 48.
9. See n. 16 on p. 49.
10. See n. 14 on p. 48.
11. See n. 15 on p. 49.

abuse or disorder committed by the slaves in this situation which continued until the Country was evacuated by the British. I was present a part of the time. The Negroes have been accused of commiting wanton Acts of cruelty during their revolt in St. Domingo, where no doubt many attrocious acts of vengance were commited on both sides but the Negroes had less in their Power than the Whites fighting on a smaller scale & with fewer means and being a war of no quarter on both sides they had fewer victims but to detail those acts of cruelty would be entirely foreign to the intention of this work. I merely wish to shew that Negroes without Law or restraint are no more to be dreaded than the lower orders of Whites under the same circumstance which I have Proved by incontravertible facts in that very Isd. of St. Domingo where after the Revolutionary flame had subsided I lived a long time at Petitgoave where often had occasion to travel backwards and forwards on horse back sometimes across all over the western & southern part of the island alone with my saddle bags full of specie. The roads through woods & over mountain were full of Negroes mostly armed and sometimes in groups of 30 or 40 who appeared to be without any restraint of law. I never was stopped or insulted by them but treated with the greatest civility throughout and hundreds of Americans can now testify to the same state of things during the Reigns of Toussant & Jean Jacques de Saline & other than I saw I don't say. history informs us that at a former period the free Colloured people of Brasil aided by the slaves drove out the Dutch; and saved that Collony. Our own History of our Revolution testifies their utility as Soldiers and the History of the later Revolutions which have taken place in South america proves two very encouraging facts to those whose fortune & property consists of slaves or in lands in those sections of our southern country such as florida where white labourers cannot on account of climate or other natural causes be substituted for the Labor of Black or Coloured people. it is this that in all their wars & Revolutions no Revolt or disturbance ever happened among the slaves or various colours or casts of People. Brasil, the most Powerfull & Populous & extensive of all European Collonies in America with a prodigious body of free collored people amalgamated with white perfectly united in fighting the Battles of their country & preserving good order among an immense body of slaves Has now become a powerfull Empire equal if not superior in natural resources to the U. States.[12] The same good fortune attended Peru where Prodigious Slave Properties were held[13] in Short there has been no Revolt or blood shed any

12. See n. 8 on p. 45.

13. In 1821, Peru began to move away from slave labor by passing a law that freed after a period of apprenticeship children born to slaves. Peru did not completely abolish slavery until

where in South America attending this kind of property which still remains as it was excepting when it was liberated by National acts of emancipation. this Proves that under moderate & prudent management it is the most permanent & indestructable of all other kinds of Property because it renews and takes care of itself and if any accident befals it we shall owe it to our own want of skill in the Science of Government. two requisites are chiefly necessary one is to treat our slaves with justice prudence & moderation. The other is to have the free Colloured Population interested in preserving peace and good order among the slaves and being firmly attached to the side of the whites by having the same Interest. this is easiest done by letting them alone and doing away every fear or idea of Tyrany & oppression or of partial taxes which to say the least of them are unconstitutional therefore unjust for we have just as great a right to make a Law to hang them for being a shade darker than our selves or for being our children as we have to drive them away by our Tyrany & oppression without having committed any crime.

We are the causes of their existence and they have natural and certain rights to that existence equal with our selves. we are not obliged to associate with them or with any one whose condition we think inferior to our own but from choice. let them go as they please and come as they please acquire property hold it & enjoy it as they Please. In short all our acts of Legislation should be confined within a proper sphere, and directed to fit objects otherwise we act against ourselves which is allways bad Pollicy never followed by sound Polliticians. If merit consisted in colour a Majority prejudiced in favor of any particular shade might drive out or exterminate the rest to make room for their favorite complexion. This would most likely depend upon what color they had been most used to as custom commonly regulates our degrees of prejudice. Ingenuity has long been racked and all its inventive faculties put in requisition to find out some way of getting entirely rid of the black & colloured population of the U. States. some Mathematicians who depended more on miracle than demonstration and who forgot to compare the bulk of the article with the means of transportation held out the plausibility of an African establishment for getting rid of this great imaginary burthen without first considering that all the suitable lands in Africa (which is a very small proportion) were already thickly settled and occupied from the earliest ages by an agricultural & economical people so that no spare room for new inhabitants existed without displacing an equal numbers of

---

1854, when the government compensated slave owners for the 25,500 slaves still in bondage. Tulio Haperín Donghi, "Economy and Society in Post-Independence Spanish America," in Leslie Bethell, ed., *The Cambridge History of Latin America*, vol. 3, *From Independence to c. 1870* (Cambridge: Cambridge University Press, 1985), 322, 341, 552–53.

old ones which could only be done by force.[14] Even if the inhabitants had been wandering Tribes like our own of North Ammerica its distance would have precluded the possibility of transportation only on a scale sufficient to answer the purposes of Colonisation & which may yet suit the object of speculation or evaporating a redundance of Missionary Zeal and scouring our Colloured population of idle vagrants which greatly needs. Had the Zealots of Colonization been serious and awake at the last evacuation of the Spanish part of St. Domingo & compromised the Right of settlements with the Haytian chiefs.[15] They then had an opportunity of securing a very respectable Colony of free colored people immediately, which certainly would have rendered that Island more formidable than it otherwise can become in many years and by cultivating the arts & Sciences have made it a much more respectable Neighbourhood than it now is; entirely dependant on a military Government for peace & protection and which It as well as all the new Governments of America needs & must have! otherwise property will not be secure. All or most Political economists are already satisfied from experiment that a secure Government of civil laws without military protection requires a very enlightened state of society to which none of those new Governments of America can arrive in many years. indeed all Governments hitherto have been supported more or less by fear & force and must be until some mechanical process of education is invented very different from the tedious complicated and expensive modes heretofore adopted. I even doubt whether Mr. Owen's progress in moral improvement at New Harmony will not be too slow to supersede the necessity of penal laws and an efficient Government for a length of time to come.[16] As the only remaining possibility of geting radically & entirely rid of the Colored people of the U. States is by exterminating the whole, we ought before we begin a Job of such

14. See n. 41 on p. 73.

15. See n. 42 on p. 74.

16. Robert Owen (1771–1858), a British social reformer and socialist, first came to the United States in December 1824. Early in 1825, Owen visited the communal colony of Harmony established by George Rapp in southwestern Indiana. In April 1825, Owen purchased the entire village and surrounding lands from Rapp and established New Harmony as a communal settlement. Hundreds of people came to the community from many states. It gained prominence as an intellectual and cultural center, attracting noted scientists, educators, and writers. Absent for two extended trips to Europe in 1825 and 1827, Owen left New Harmony for the final time in June 1828. Individualism and dissension among members of the community ended the enterprise by 1828, though the town of New Harmony remained. Arthur Eugene Bestor, Jr., *Backwoods Utopias: The Sectarian and Owenite Phases of Communitarian Socialism in America, 1663–1829* (Philadelphia, Pa.: 1950); J. F. C. Harrison, *Robert Owen and the Owenites in Britain and America: The Quest for a New Moral World* (London: Routledge and Kegan Paul, 1969), 105–6, 163–65.

importance (for they constitute fully one sixth part of our whole population) consider well how far the approbation of our own citizens and that of lookers on would go along with us and be well assured that we are on the strong side before we begin. otherwise our situation might be dangerous, as we may see by the cause of the Turks & Greeks now before us how far the World can be led by prejudice.[17] Let us even suppose that we can get rid of our own colored population some way or other; Again we look round and see still a greater difficulty to be overcome. For all around us which ever way we turn our faces, colored people still exist, so numerous that perhaps two thirds of all the remaining population of America is more or less composed of them. Whole Armies of Negroes & black Generals from whom we receive Embassadors and with whom we are already linked by Commercial Treaties! We must either continue to be on friendly terms with all these people and treat them as they treat us or we must be in a state of hostility and shut ourselves up in our Forrests & mountains like the Chinese, we would have no commerce for we should have the whole world against us therefore no place to trade to! Florida without mountains and all sea bord would be badly off. Even the Island of Hytie of which Neighbour we entertain so poor an opinion would ruin us by blockading our Ports and carrying off our slaves by force, if we were not shielded by the Respectability of the Government of the U. States of which we fortunately are a member. In short there is no back door for us to get out at, we are fixed in Florida with the sea on both sides. We must have slaves to cultivate our lands and free colored people are a necessary consequence of having slaves. we cannot have the one without having the other and we must be there ourselves and do the best we can with them both. If any word, sentence, or allusion in the smallest degree offends any person who reads the foregoing treatise I do assure them that no Offense was intended but merely an investigation of Facts the consideration of which it was hoped might promote the welfare & happiness of the people of Florida.

Z. Kingsley

17. The Greek War of Independence began in 1821, as the Greeks tried to gain their independence from the Ottoman Empire. Europeans overwhelmingly favored the Greek cause, and in 1826 Russia and England agreed to mediate between the Greeks and Turks. However, the Ottoman Empire refused an armistice, Russia declared war on Turkey, and allied forces defeated the Turks. The Ottoman Empire was forced to accept the Treaty of Adrianople in 1829, which ended the war with Russia and recognized Greek independence. European nations recognized Greek independence in 1832.

Letter to the Editor of
the *East Florida Herald* (1826)[1]

FOR THE HERALD.

The single object of the author of the following essay, is to encrease the value of southern possessions. To do this it is all important, that the persons and property of the whites, should be rendered more secure and permanent, 1st by attaching the Free people of color to their interest & 2dly by propitiating the better feelings of the enlightened world, now enlisted against that species of property called negro slaves, so necessary and indispensable, from the nature of our climate of our soil.

It is on the permanent security of this species of property that the present, as well as the future, prosperity and value of all Southern possessions depend. I submit it then to the People and to the Council of this Territory, whether these objects (such as these) do not merit mature consideration? and their perfect or partial attainment shall be purposes of the following observations.

No subject has excited a deeper interest throughout every section of the union, than its colored population. The modes proposed to rid ourselves of what is deemed an incumbrance are so various. The arguments by which each is supported so multifarious and comprehensive, that it would be idle to advance a new hypothesis; and yet they are so variant & so contradictory

---

1. Printed Letter. *East Florida Herald* (St. Augustine, Fla.), December 12, 1826. This letter is the first of at least two and probably four or five letters published in the *East Florida Herald* over the pen name "Rationalis." The second letter with the title "To the Legislative Council of the Floridas" appeared in the December 26, 1826, issue. It promised future articles on the same topic, but those issues of the *East Florida Herald* have not survived. It seems probable that Kingsley or the editor of the newspaper rewrote portions of his "Address to the Legislative Council of Florida" into a series of four or five articles that the newspaper then published, while the Legislative Council was in session in Tallahassee.

that it would be worse than idle to attempt to reconcile them. [(]But so violent and acrimonious has the controversy now become that some decisive step is indispensable, for the preservation of our southern property, which must necessarily rise or fall in value, as this subject is disposed of with rashness or discretion.)—There is no stock in the U. States, in which capital, can be so profitably invested, as in a southern farm worked by well managed negros. Our lands are rich and low priced, and convenient to the water: and our crops are sugar, and Sea Island Cotton and Oranges, articles of all others the most productive to the planter, and the most remote from northern competition. But so strong is the belief with monied men to the north that this kind of property could never be rendered permanently secure, that they have hitherto been absolutely deterred from embarking in the experiment. I consider that this apprehension of theirs, and the consequent low prices of our Land and negros, arises from our own mismanagement and want of policy in the enactment of laws regulating this species of our population. Rewards as well as punishments are the great stimulant, to rectitude of conduct—but we have lost sight of all but the punishments. Hope and self interest, are not enlisted, even as auxiliaries to fear and oppression—the sole engines of our laws. It is thus, that by a natural consequence, the affections of the free persons of color, [a] great and growing portion of our people[,] is alienated from the Whites. It is thus that many of our farmers are alarmed, and have glutted the market with their slaves. It is thus that northern capitalists are taught to fear, not only for the investments they might be induced to make, but for their own personal life and safety.

Our Territory is unrivalled in the advantages of its locality. It is washed by an ocean on its full extent; nature has given us a market to the East and to the West. We are blest with a climate to which the healthy may resort for pleasure and the invalid for health, with a soil that teems with all the fruit of the Tropics, and repays by its product to a four fold amount the labors of the husbandmen and yet there is no portion of the Union, where money is so scarce, and distress and poverty so universally prevailing. Our lands are without value—& unless some exertion is made for us a change is not likely to become an amendment, at least until we remove the present prejudice, against the property in slaves, arising from a general belief in its insecurity. That this security is all important will be at once conceded. That it is possible, nay perfectly practicable, I think I shall be able to shew. Some indeed, believe that this is a subject too delicate for public discussion—but I doubt that policy which shrinks from a rigid investigation. How are we to cure the evils that oppress us, without understanding their nature and their causes.

Liberty is an empty name, where we fear to speak boldly, and in the language of the immortal Jefferson, error alone shrinks from the test of reason and of truth.[2]

RATIONALIS

2. This reference is perhaps to Jefferson's first inaugural address, delivered on March 4, 1801: "error of opinion may be tolerated where reason is left free to combat it."
For Jefferson's attitude toward slavery, see Miller, *The Wolf by the Ears.*

A Treatise on the Patriarchal, or Co-operative System of Society (1828–1934)[1]

A
Treatise
on
The Patriarchal[,
or
Co-operative[1828, 1829]] System of Society,
As it Exists in Some Governments,
And Colonies in America, and in the United States,
Under
The Name of Slavery,
With its Necessity and Advantages.
By an Inhabitant of Florida.
[1828.]
[Second Edition.[1829]]
[1829.]
[Third Edition, With an Appendix.[1833]]
[1833.]
[Fourth Edition, With an Appendix.[1834]]
[1834.]

Preface.

It will be allowed by every one, that agriculture is the great foundation of the
wealth and prosperity of our Southern States. This important science has
already attracted some share of attention from men of the first talents, by
whose improvements in cultivation several valuable productions promise,
from their superiority, to maintain a preference in Foreign markets; and the

1. Printed Document.

recent introduction of new articles of tropical produce into the [more[1828]] southern districts, where they bid fair to succeed, offers still greater incitements to agricultural enterprise, and opens a new and extensive range for future speculation.

While this great field of wealth and independence promises now to be well understood and duly appreciated, the primary cause and means by which alone it can be realized, has either escaped attention, or been designedly overlooked: I mean the perpetuation of that kind of labor which now produces it, and which seems best adapted, under all circumstances, to render it profitable to the Southern capitalist.

The idea of slavery, when associated with cruelty and injustice, is revolting to every philanthropic mind; but when that idea is associated with justice and benevolence, slavery, commonly so called, easily amalgamates with the ordinary conditions of life.

To counteract the existing prejudices against slavery, by making it evident that the condition of slaves may be equally happy and more independent of the ordinary evils of life, than that of the common class of whites denominated free—that they are now equally virtuous, moral, and less corrupted than the ordinary class of laboring whites;—that their labor is far more productive—that they yield more support and benefit to the State, which, under a well regulated system of management, is better fitted to endure a state of war than it would be with an equal number of free white people of ordinary means and condition; and, finally, that the Slave or Patriarchal System of Society (so often commiserated as a subject of deep regret) which constitutes the bond of social compact of the Southern seaboard of the United States, is better adapted for strength, durability, and independence, than any other state of society hitherto adopted. To endeavor to prove all this, and to destroy the prejudice existing against slavery, under the circumstances with which it is now associated in the South, is the object of the present Essay; dedicated to the people of Florida, and to political economists[2] throughout the Southern States, by a votary of rational policy, and most respectfully their humble servant. (1)

[Z. Kingsley.[1828, 1829, 1833]]
[A Slave Holder.[1834]]

2. Kingsley was only one of several proslavery writers who utilized the science of political economy to assess aspects of slavery. Drew Gilpin Faust has argued that neglected southern intellectuals publicly justified slavery to enhance their social roles in southern culture. Drew Gilpin Faust, "A Southern Stewardship: The Intellectual and the Proslavery Argument," *American Quarterly* 31 (spring 1979): 63–80; Tise, *Proslavery,* 64–69.

A Treatise
on
The Patriarchal Slave System.

That there is a large portion of territory in the Southern states unfavorable to the health and production of white people, is evident from the sickly appearance of nearly the whole seaboard laboring white population, extending from [the[1833, 1834]] Chesapeake Bay to the Mississippi. This sickly appearance is most observed among the lower orders, who are exposed to the weather; and it can only be accounted for by supposing that nature has not fitted a white complexion for hard work in the sun, as it is evident that the darkness of complexion here is a measure of capacity for endurance of labor, under that influence.

Many, from a superficial view of things, suppose that the aversion to labor, observable in the South, among the working classes of whites, proceeds from natural indisposition. But a nearer view, and better acquaintance with facts will show, that the radical cause is the want of health, which produces an apathy or aversion to work, and frequently a relaxation, or want of natural excitement in the powers of life, which seek artificial stimulants; as we see frequent instances of the strongest, soberest, and most industrious mechanics coming from the North, becoming, after a few years hard labor, weak and idle, and finally, falling a sacrifice to the abuse of ardent spirits. Some are of opinion, that the want of health in these classes, is owing to their being unaccustomed to a hot climate. But as many years have elapsed since the first white people settled among the Southern swamps, and their descendants have not improved either in looks or longevity, it becomes evident that people of white complexions are unfitted by nature for that situation. (2)

Some of our Northern neighbors, living in a state of health and affluence, and not being aware that this prosperous state, in many instances, proceeds indirectly from Southern slave labour, and without duly investigating, and comparing the hardships, and humiliation of the lower condition of their white population with the more comfortable state of the Southern negroes, have denounced the patriarchal state of subordination of the latter, called slavery, as the most abject and miserable of all possible grades of human existence. Now it appears to me, that no one state can be perfectly free from these evils; but that all must experience some modifications of dependence.(3) The negro, under the management of a just, conscientious, and humane master; (of which description it will certainly be allowed that there are some) who provides for the physical wants of his servants, his wife and children, in health, sickness and old age, for no other consideration than the equitable one of competent labor, when in health, will surely enjoy a happier and more enviable state of existence than the poor white man, burdened with a family, who has to contend with cold and hunger, besides religious and moral tyranny.

Moreover, the free white man, with the greatest economy and industry, usually consumes nearly the whole product of his labor; laying by but little, even under the most favorable circumstances, but with a smaller stock of prudence and exertion, which more commonly happens, he not only consumes all his earnings, but is compelled by cold, hunger, and want of employment or ill health, to apply to the public for charity. Whereas the negro by his [own[1828]] labor, discreetly restrained under the [co-operative, or[1828, 1829]] Patriarchal system, not only furnishes clothing, implements of husbandry, and provision, but creates a large export surplus to meet contingencies; thus increasing the comfort and capital of the establishment, of which he considers himself an integral part. (4)

In short, the greatest value of agricultural [produce[1828]] [product[1829, 1833, 1834]] for export, and nearly all the springs of national and individual prosperity, flow from slave labor, as is fairly demonstrated by our annual account of exports.[3] It could not reasonably be expected otherwise. The labor of the negro, under the wholesome restraint of an intelligent direction, is like a constant stream; that of the white man is economically measured out by his urgent necessities, or dissipated by his expenses. Besides, climate enables the one to furnish articles of greater value; while the white man's labor is usually applied to raise cheap articles of food for the mere subsistence of himself and family.

Such is the comparative usefulness of these two classes of society in our present state of peace. But to render a slave holding country stronger, and equally advantageous in a state of war, against which it ought always to be prepared; or, in other words, to neutralize the spirit of disaffection which necessarily results from every unequal distribution of privileges; it will be requisite to alter a little our present policy. (5) Before, however, we begin, and by way of getting rid of some slight prejudices, it might be well to take

---

3. South Carolina Governor Stephen D. Miller used similar language in his speech to the state legislature in 1829: "The agricultural wealth of the country is found in those states owning slaves, and a great portion of the revenue of the government is derived from the products of slave labor." *Charleston Courier,* November 28, 1829.

a view of some other slave holding countries, which have already undergone the test of experiment, and successfully resisted all the disorganizing temptations and insidious machinations of powerful, but, as yet, unsuccessful enemies; (6) and endeavor to obtain safe and conclusive evidence from established precedents exactly applicable to our [own[1828]] circumstances.

First, I will take a view of Brazil, (7) which is by far the most powerful and extensive slave holding country in America, or in the world; its population consists of something less than one million of whites, something more than one million of free colored, and considerably over two millions of slaves[, besides many independent Indian nations[1834]].[4] It passed through such a war of revolution as our own, from the colonial state to that of an independent government, attended with all the violence of conflicting interests, opinions, and consequent hostility of royal and independent partizans, with their hostile armies. It now ranks, as Empire of Brazil, perhaps the most extensive government in the world, and is carrying on war with the Free Republic of Buenos Ayres; with its white and free colored population, it has fitted out, manned, and sent to sea, nearly forty ships of war, and has raised or sent to the frontiers, nearly fifty thousand regular troops. It now affords the grand imposing spectacle of a slave holding government, whose population greatly preponderates in favor of color, at war with a free Re-

---

4. Although there are few reliable population statistics for Brazilian society from the mid-eighteenth to the mid-nineteenth centuries, Kingsley seems to have been roughly accurate. Estimates for the racial composition of Brazil in 1810 are 28 percent whites, 27.8 percent free blacks and mulattoes, 38.1 percent slave blacks and mulattoes, and 5.7 percent Indians. In Brazil as a whole, the number of free people of color (including Indians) surpassed that of whites, though slaves made up the largest percentage of the population. When it gained its independence from Portugal in 1822, Brazil had a population of between four and five million, including approximately 800,000 Brazilian Indians. The best estimate for the total number of slaves is 1,147,515 in 1823. In the early 1820s, Brazil was importing 30,000 slaves annually. Leslie Bethell, ed., *Colonial Brazil* (Cambridge: Cambridge University Press, 1987), 290; Leslie Bethell and José Murilo de Carvalho, "Brazil from Independence to the Middle of the Nineteenth Century," in Bethell, ed., *The Cambridge History of Latin America*, 3:679–80.
The race and status of the population varied considerably among Brazilian provinces, as three-fourths of the slaves lived in only five of the eighteen provinces. In one of these—the mining captaincy of Minas Gerais—surviving statistics for 1821 enumerate 136,693 whites (27 percent), 152,921 free mulattoes (30 percent), 53,719 free blacks (10 percent), 22,788 slave mulattoes (4 percent), and 148,416 slave blacks (29 percent). Therefore, free people of color constituted the largest segment of society (40 percent) in this area of colonial Brazil. A. J. R. Russell-Wood, *The Black Man in Slavery and Freedom in Colonial Brazil* (London: Macmillan Press, 1982), 49.

public, which constitutionally disavows slavery,[5] and which not only endeavors to subdue it by force of arms, but to subvert it by inflammatory proclamations: offering freedom and protection to the slaves as their reward for revolt. But all these disorganizing temptations have heretofore failed; the slaves maintain their obligation, and do their work peaceably as usual; furnishing produce and means, not only to support the national credit, but to carry on the war, and repel the bearers of these insidious proclamations. This trait of virtue and fidelity in the Brazilian slaves is to be attributed to humane and just treatment.[6]

The door of liberty is open to every slave who can find the means of purchasing himself.[7] It is true, few have the means, but hope creates a spirit of economy, industry, and emulation to obtain merit by good behavior, which has a general and beneficial effect. Slaves are also allowed to hold some kinds of property, under limitation—such as stock. But the grand chain of security by which the slaves are held in subordination, is the free people of color, whose persons, properties, and rights are protected by law; which enables them to acquire and hold property in their own name, and allows the free children of quarteroons by a white man, to be white by law.

5. The Republic of Buenos Aires did not abolish slavery officially until the adoption of the Constitution of 1853. Slavery survived through an illegal slave trade, which the government openly tolerated. Many slaves gained emancipation through military service in the wars of independence. Slavery was especially prevalent in the cities; in 1822, 12 percent of the inhabitants of the city of Buenos Aires were slaves. John Lynch, "The River Plate Republics from Independence to the Paraguayan War," in Bethell, ed., The Cambridge History of Latin America, 3:639–40.

6. The war between Brazil and the Republic of Buenos Aires stemmed from a longstanding Spanish and Portuguese rivalry over the Banda Oriental, the area of modern Uruguay. In 1816 Portuguese troops from Brazil occupied the area during the Spanish American wars of independence. In 1821 the area was incorporated into Brazil as the Cisplatine Province. In October 1825, the Republic of Buenos Aires took advantage of a rebellion in the area to claim the Banda Oriental as part of the United Provinces of the Río de la Plata. This action amounted to a declaration of war, and Brazil reciprocated six weeks later. Contrary to Kingsley's positive portrait, the war went disastrously for Brazil. Although far superior to Argentine forces on paper, the Brazilian troops were repeatedly defeated. Plagued by poor leadership, inadequate supplies, corruption, disease, and a high desertion rate, the Brazilian army never gained an advantage over their adversaries. Ron Seckinger, The Brazilian Monarchy and the South American Republics, 1822–1831: Diplomacy and State Building (Baton Rouge: Louisiana State University Press, 1984), 59–73.

7. Though more common in Brazil than in the United States, manumission through purchase was not a legal right granted to Brazilian slaves. Carl N. Degler, Neither Black Nor White: Slavery and Race Relations in Brazil and the United States (New York: Macmillan, 1971), 39–47.

By this link, they become identified with the whites on one side, and with the slaves by descent on the other; a connexion which perfectly cements the three castes of which the whole nation is composed; and each being perfectly contented with its permanent, lawful privileges, the jealousy, which might otherwise arise from caste or difference of complexion or condition, is totally extinguished, and no one feels an interest in disturbing that with which every one is satisfied.[8]

The British colonial policy is fast verging to the same point. Its object is to improve the education and mental attainments of its free colored population, as well as to protect its slaves from unjust oppression.

The free colored people are thus gradually rendered fit to take place of the whites, whose lives have long been uselessly sacrificed to a hot climate, which does not, nor ever can agree with them. They have so far progressed, as to fill up a great deal of agricultural as well as mercantile room, and most of the militia troops with free colored people, who are good mechanics, well educated, and of great respectability; so that a very considerable share of landed property has already passed into their hands. Their law also entitles

8. Kingsley's characterization of the legal status of free people of color in Brazil was idealized. Although they did enjoy more economic and social mobility than their counterparts in the United States, free people of color in Brazil faced discriminatory legislation, which frequently made no distinction between slaves and freedmen. Neither free people of color nor slaves, for example, could carry weapons or wear certain types of clothing. Penalties for legal infractions were also harsher for people of color, free or slave, than for whites. Perhaps the mediating role of free people of color in Brazil, as praised by Kingsley, had less to do with their identification of self-interest with whites than with antagonisms and divisions within the black community. The ambiguous status of free people of color in Brazil is evident in the fact that *"de jure* standing did not necessarily correspond to everyday reality and . . . a *de facto* position often had no basis in law." Russell-Wood, *Black Man in Slavery and Freedom,* 67–82, 203; Herbert S. Klein, "The Colored Freedmen in Brazilian Slave Society," *Journal of Social History* 3 (fall 1969): 30–52.

In his study of Bahia, a major plantation zone on the coast of central Brazil, Stuart B. Schwartz asserts that although free blacks and mulattoes as well as slaves were involved in social and political unrest between 1790 and 1837, they rarely united their efforts. The differences between crioulos and Africans and between blacks and mulattoes were important categories of distinction: "Divided by color and place of birth, by juridical status and hope of improvement, slaves and free people of color did not for the most part make common cause." Colonial Brazilian slave society "had created a set of racial and status divisions that effectively interdicted cooperation." The war against slavery in Bahia after 1798 was conducted "almost exclusively by African slaves and by those freed persons of African birth for whom ethnicity was more vital than judicial status." Stuart B. Schwartz, *Sugar Plantations in the Formation of Brazilian Society: Bahia, 1550–1835* (Cambridge: Cambridge University Press, 1985), 472–79.

the children of free quarteroons to all white privileges, if the father is white.[9] By this policy they unite the two castes, who become equally interested in maintaining good order and contentment among the slaves.[10]

The Spanish, French, and Dutch Colonies have all adopted the same policy.[11]

9. Kingsley may here have overstated British policy by one generation. The children of quadroons/quarteroons were three generations removed from a black ancestor, but those entitled "by birth to all the rights and liberties of White subjects in the full extent are such as are above three steps removed in lineal digression from the Negro Venter." Children four generations removed from a black ancestor had one black and fifteen white great-great grandparents, hardly a liberal provision as Kingsley here characterizes it. Bryan Edwards, *The History, Civil and Commercial, of the West Indies* (London, 1793), vol. 2, bk. 4, p. 17, quoted in Douglas Hall, "Jamaica," in Cohen and Greene, eds., *Neither Slave Nor Free,* 196.

10. The major British colonies early in the nineteenth century were Jamaica and Barbados, though the British also governed the British Windward Islands, the British Leeward Islands, Trinidad, Tobago, the Bahamas, and the Cayman Islands. In Barbados in 1828, free people of color comprised only 5 percent, whites 15 percent, and slaves 80 percent of the population. During the same period in other British colonies, such as Jamaica, free people of color outnumbered whites, but slaves remained a large majority of the population. Racial discrimination in the legal system of British colonies had become more rigid during the eighteenth century as free people of color were deprived of their rights to hold employment in public offices, vote, purchase or inherit more than modest sums, testify in courts, or navigate coastal vessels. Various acts between 1817 and 1831 removed legal discrimination against free people of color in the British colonies. Although slavery was abolished in British possessions in the 1830s, caste distinctions remained and whites still held the reins of power. Hall, "Jamaica," 193–213; and Jerome S. Handler and Arnold A. Sio, "Barbados," in Cohen and Greene, eds., *Neither Slave Nor Free,* 214–57.

11. The principal Spanish colonies were Cuba, Mexico, Puerto Rico, Panama, and most of the colonies in South America. In these colonies, the number of free blacks and mulattoes grew throughout the colonial period. By the nineteenth century, free people of color outnumbered slaves in most Spanish colonies. In 1820 in Puerto Rico, whites comprised 44 percent, free people of color 46 percent, and slaves 9 percent of the population. Even in Cuba, a bastion of slavery, free people of color in 1827 constituted 27 percent of the nonwhite population. Their legal status was considerably better than that of slaves, but inferior to that of Spaniards and Indians. Prejudice limited educational opportunities and therefore access to the bureaucracy and the professions. However, free people of color were well represented in the arts and crafts, as well as in militia service. The upward social mobility of free blacks and mulattoes prevented them from identifying with the slaves beneath them. Legal disabilities for free people of color in Spanish colonies generally ended with independence. Frederick P. Bowser, "Colonial Spanish America," and Franklin W. Knight, "Cuba," in Cohen and Greene, eds., *Neither Slave Nor Free,* 19–58, 284.

Major French colonies included the French Antilles (Martinique, Guadeloupe, Grenada), French Guiana, and Saint Domingue. Although the *Code Noir* of 1685 granted free people of color equal rights with whites, prejudices remained, and legal proscriptions against free blacks increased between 1730 and 1780. They were excluded from certain occupations, segregated in theaters and churches, taxed more heavily, and forbidden to intermarry with whites. Some of these restrictions eased on Martinique in the 1820s, and the ban on intermarriage was

The island of Saint Domingo is now independent under its aboriginal name Hayti. (8) Its colonial tranquility was first disturbed by national edicts, which the French people, while frantic with revolutionary zeal, madly promulgated in their colonies. This dangerous fanaticism soon spread itself among the slave holders, who being divided in[to[1828, 1829]] two great political factions, nearly equal in strength, armed their slaves to support their own political opinions. This, together with their pride in denying the participation of equality to the free colored people,[12] caused the destruction of that flourishing and important colony. The fall, and final extinction of its colonial power, and its subsequent re-establishment under a free and independent government of negroes in our vicinity, furnishes in a variety of incidents which took place during its whole course, abundant examples of situation, occurrences, and facts, from which we may establish conse-

---

abolished in 1830. In 1826 free people of color made up approximately 10 percent of the population of Martinique; whites accounted for another 10 percent, and slaves were the remaining 80 percent. Over the next decade, liberal manumission provisions tripled the size of the free black group, which then constituted 25 percent of the total population. Enactments in 1830 and 1832 ended legal discrimination against free people of color in the French colonies. As in other colonies, free blacks tried to forge alliances with the white ruling class rather than with the slaves. Only after 1830 did some free people of color join the antislavery struggle, seeing their oppression as linked to the continuance of slavery. Léo Elisabeth, "The French Antilles," in Cohen and Greene, eds., *Neither Slave Nor Free,* 134–71.

Dutch colonies included Surinam on the northeast coast of South America, the Netherlands Antilles (including Curaçao, Aruba, and Bonaire) near the coast of Venezuela, and three small islands in the northeastern corner of the Caribbean archipelago (Saint Eustatius, Saba, half of St. Martin). In the sugar colony of Surinam in 1830, free people of color comprised nearly 9 percent and slaves more than 86 percent of the population. Governor Wichers, during his tenure (1784–90), encouraged manumission and pursued a deliberate policy of placing free people of color in the middle levels of the social structure. In the early decades of the nineteenth century, however, manumission became more difficult. Manumitted slaves had to pay a fee to the government. In 1825 slaves were forbidden to buy their own freedom, and after 1832, slaves had to be a member of an officially recognized religious institution to be eligible for manumission. In the commercial colony of Curaçao in 1833, whites formed 17 percent, free people of color 43 percent, and slaves 39 percent of the total population. The colonial government of Curaçao also limited manumissions early in the nineteenth century. Legislation in 1813 stipulated that freed slaves would not receive their civil rights until two years after manumission. Despite restrictions, manumissions remained frequent in both Surinam and Curaçao, and neither society prohibited interracial marriages. H. Hoetink, "Surinam and Curaçao," in Cohen and Greene, eds., *Neither Slave Nor Free,* 59–83.

12. By the 1780s Saint Domingue had a large, wealthy community of free blacks, but they were bound by harsh laws. Thomas O. Ott, *The Haitian Revolution, 1789–1804* (Knoxville, Tenn.: University of Tennessee Press, 1973), 3–21; David Patrick Geggus, *Slavery, War and Revolution: The British Occupation of Saint Domingue, 1793–1798* (Oxford: Oxford University Press, 1982), 18–23.

quences that would apply to almost every possible situation in which we could imagine slaves of a similar class to our own to be placed.

To infuse a general spirit of revolt among the numerous plantations of St. Domingo, appears to have been a matter which required both time and labor to accomplish; especially as some departments were more prudent than others, and tried to counteract it. Santhonax and Polvorel,[13] the commissioners sent out from France to enforce the national decrees of liberty and equality, were the most active and successful propagators of liberty. But in many of the quarters, the slaves still continued to work, even without white overseers, and furnished large quantities of coffee for exportation during the whole government of Toussaint.[14] And, what is still more remarkable, the rich and extensive department of Grande Anse continued to furnish nearly its usual quantity of produce, and remained quiet for several

13. Léger Félicité Sonthonax (1763–1813) and Etienne Polverel (1738–95) were sent by the French revolutionary government to the French colony of Saint Domingue in July 1792. Their first task, ironically similar to Kingsley's goals in Florida forty years later, was to enforce the Law of 4 April, which guaranteed full civil equality to free men of color. Soon, Sonthonax's own abolitionist beliefs led him to push for more radical measures. In August 1793, Sonthonax proclaimed the Declaration of the Rights of Man and Citizen in the North province of Saint Domingue, thereby eliminating slavery. In 1794, the two commissioners were arrested by order of the National Convention and returned to France. In 1795, the commissioners were vindicated of the charges against them, and Sonthonax returned as an agent of the Directory in May 1796. Hoping to establish a new regime in Saint Domingue, Sonthonax became deeply embroiled in the internal conflicts in the colony. In August 1797, Toussaint Louverture expelled Sonthonax from Saint Domingue, and the latter returned to France. Robert Louis Stein, *Léger Félicité Sonthonax: The Lost Sentinel of the Republic* (Cranbury, N.J.: Associated University Presses, 1985), 41–42, 104–6, 123–24, 170.

14. Toussaint Louverture (c. 1744–1803) was a self-educated slave freed before the slave uprising in Saint Domingue in August 1791. He joined the rebellion and eventually became the political and military leader of the French colony. He successfully drove the British off the island in 1798 and quelled a revolt by free blacks against his rule in 1799. In 1801 he conquered Santo Domingo, ceded by Spain to France in 1795, and governed the whole island. Louverture organized a meeting to write a new constitution in 1801. The Constitution of 1801 made Louverture governor general for life, and although professing nominal allegiance to France, the new constitution made Saint Domingue virtually independent. Angered by such a display of independence, Napoleon Bonaparte in 1802 sent a large expedition under General Charles Victor Emmanuel Leclerc to subdue the colonists. The Haitians resisted stubbornly, and a peace treaty was signed in May. In June 1802, the French arrested Louverture and sent him to France, where he died in a dungeon. He became a symbol of the fight for liberty to some and of the dangers of black self-rule to others. See C. L. R. James, *The Black Jacobins: Toussaint L'Ouverture and the San Domingo Revolution*, 2d ed. (New York: Vintage Books, 1989), and Ott, *The Haitian Revolution*.

years after the commencement of the revolution, and until Jeremie was evacuated by the British, notwithstanding that this department was annually besieged by Generals Toussaint and Rigaud,[15] commanding the armies of the [South[1828, 1829, 1833]] [North[1834]] and of the West, accompanied by all their seditious proclamations. The slaves were armed by their masters, and protected themselves and families while they made abundant crops of coffee.[16] In short, when we come to consider the massacres and bloodshed necessarily attending such a horrid revolution, where a vast number of slaves were forced into a state of licentious anarchy, and led on by partizans blinded by revolutionary fury, who gave no quarter on either side, it is astonishing that the slaves now liberated should have so soon returned to a peaceable and quiet state of domestic order, and again admitted whites to reside peaceably among them, and enjoy all the pre-eminence that condition could give. (9) But such was the fact; and considering that they were still acting on the defensive against the British, who, for many years after, and with all their disposable force, endeavored to subdue them, it is a matter of astonishment and wonder how so much produce was still made as was exported under the reign of Toussaint, and until the arrival of the grand French expedition under Rochambeau and Leclerc, in (1802–3) when the island was again thrown into anarchy, and would have been ultimately reconquered but for the breaking out of the war afresh between France and Britain, which suspended the farther progress of the conquest, and finally

15. André Rigaud (1761–1811) was a general and leader of the free black caste in the South province of Saint Domingue. Initially an ally of Toussaint Louverture in the North against a common British enemy, the relationship between Louverture and Rigaud erupted into open warfare in 1799. After a year of civil warfare, Louverture's forces subdued the South, and forced Rigaud into exile in France. In 1802 Rigaud returned with General Leclerc's expedition in another attempt to wrest power from Louverture.

16. La Grand' Anse was a coffee-growing region at the western tip of the southern peninsula of Saint Domingue. After the French Republic declared war on Great Britain in February 1793, the first area of Saint Domingue to surrender to the English was la Grand' Anse. White planters there had governed themselves for nearly two years, kept their slaves on the plantations, and had suppressed or driven out free blacks. However, André Rigaud's army of slaves and mulattoes threatened to subdue the entire region. From 1793 to 1798, British forces occupied the area from its principal town, Jérémie. Throughout the British occupation, la Grand' Anse exported more than 15,000,000 lbs. of coffee per year. Local planters, "patriarchs on a small scale," were among the first in Saint Domingue to arm their own slaves. For an examination of the British occupation of Saint Domingue, see Geggus, *Slavery, War and Revolution*, esp. 65, 235–36.

confirmed its independence.[17] Its government has now settled under the form of a military Republic; but the quantity of produce raised bears but little proportion to what it was under the Patriarchal restraint of its Colonial system of government, as the present state of individual emancipation implies less necessity for hard work, especially in a healthy, fertile, and mild climate such as Hayti, where few clothes are required, and bountiful nature produces spontaneously the necessaries of life.[18]

From all these facts it follows, that, under a just and prudent system of management, negroes are a safe, permanent, productive and growing property, and easily governed; that they are not naturally desirous of change, but are sober, discreet, honest and obliging; are less troublesome, and possess a [much better[1828, 1829, 1833]] moral character [than the ordinary class of corrupted whites of similar condition[1828, 1829, 1833]] [equally respectable with the ordinary class of whites[1834]]. (10)

Their strong attachment to their homes, to their [women[1828]] [wives[1829, 1833, 1834]] and children, and to domestic life, are likewise great securities for their good behavior; which, with a fair and equitable allowance of clothes and provisions, kind treatment when sick, and fair words when well, will, in most cases, insure good behavior, obedience and attachment. Under [these[1828, 1829, 1833]] [those[1834]] circumstances they will, without grumbling, and with very little corporeal punishment, perform a great deal of valuable labor in [a[1828, 1829, 1833]] [one[1834]] year, and with profit and satisfaction to the owner, who, if prudent, will soon find himself in easy circumstances, and feel happy in experiencing the attachment, confidence, and good will of a grateful and happy people. (11)

The policy generally pursued by our own slave holding state governments with regard to free colored people, and that pursued by foreign colo-

17. Donatien Marie Joseph Rochambeau served in a variety of positions for the French Empire: interim governor general of Saint Domingue (1792), governor of Martinique (1793), and commander in chief of Santo Domingo, ceded by the Spanish to the French in 1795 (1796). Charles Victor Emmanuel Leclerc (1772–1802), a French general, was one of Napoleon Bonaparte's lieutenants and his brother-in-law. In February 1802, he led a French force to subdue the colony of Saint Domingue. After achieving several costly victories, the French reached an agreement with Louverture in May. Leclerc, however, broke the treaty, seized Louverture, and deported him to France in June. Outraged, the ex-slaves under the leadership of Jean-Jacques Dessalines rose in revolt against the French led by Rochambeau, who had replaced Leclerc, a victim of a yellow fever epidemic. With the outbreak of warfare in Europe between France and Britain, Rochambeau received no reinforcements, and the French withdrew late in 1803. On January 1, 1804, Dessalines proclaimed the independence of Haiti, and in 1805 proclaimed himself Emperor. Ott, *The Haitian Revolution*, 139–87.

18. Kingsley's interpretation of Haiti's recent history here explains his satisfaction with the 1826 Rural Code of Haiti that made agricultural labor compulsory. See p. 86.

nial and other slave holding governments, is directly opposite. In the latter, the free colored people have found it their interest universally and decidedly to place themselves in the scale of the whites, or in opposition to the slaves.(12) In the former, necessity, from the unfavorable construction of the laws, has compelled them universally to throw themselves into the scale of the slaves in opposition to the whites. This difference of policy adopted by these different governments, who have precisely the same views and interests to favor, and the same objects to guard against, is obviously owing to the difference of local circumstances, growing out of the different situations of the two countries with regard to population [and government[1833, 1834]].

In our greatest slave holding states which take the lead, the great majority of [the[1828, 1829, 1833]] [our[1834]] inhabitants is white, who boast of enjoying every privilege of free men, but possessing a strong feeling of prejudice against every other shade of color, and inhabiting a high, healthy country, suitable to the labor of white people, to whom colored labor is not absolutely necessary. This majority has the right of forming [the[1833, 1834]] laws to govern the minority, or slave holding part of these states, lying nearest [to[1834]] the sea, to whom a colored population is absolutely necessary, and with the safety and good government of which a smaller degree of prejudice against color would better comport. But as the great quantity of whites in the up country is at all times ready to put down or exterminate all the colored people in case of insurrection, fear and force in governing these people are safely substituted for wisdom and policy. (14)[19]

The operation of physical causes has induced the foreign slave holding colonies and governments to adopt a policy diametrically opposite. Their climates being unfavorable to the increase of the whites, has thrown a great majority into the scale of the free colored people, many of whom, being rich and liberally educated, enjoy great respectability, and having the same interest with the whites, and great influence with the slaves, form a barrier to insurrection; which not only makes life and property safe in time of peace, but renders the whole physical strength of the country completely disposable in time of war.

North Carolina, by the liberal provisions of her constitution and enlightened policy to her free colored people, stands firmer with regard to slave

19. This number refers to the thirteenth note in the work; however, the first edition misnumbered the note as "14," and the error was perpetuated through each subsequent edition. The persistence of this error suggests that later editions were typeset from earlier ones, perhaps with deletions and insertions marked. Another possibility is that Kingsley or the printer deliberately left out the number thirteen for superstitious reasons.

property than any state to the south, not even excepting Louisiana.[20] A general line of limitation might be drawn between white and colored, such as exists in the British West India colonies. Taxes in all cases should be equal; and the law both criminal and civil should be as impartial as the sun. If it is otherwise, what kind of protection can be given either to person or [to[1833]] property; and what [must be[1828, 1829, 1833]] [is[1834]] the final result where neither is given?

I believe no disadvantage has ever been perceived in North Carolina from its free citizens of color being allowed to vote.[21]

It appears from the above statement, that to raise the value of southern plantation property to its just scale of purchase value, according to the rate of interest yielded by its neat average return of crops, to bear an equal proportion with the value and returns of real property in the north, which is the principal [object[1828, 1829, 1833]] of this treatise, it may be considered necessary—

1st. To put all fear of danger, either to person or property, from insurrection of the slaves, at rest.

2d. To destroy all doubt of the permanent durability of such property in case of war or invasion.

---

20. Although free blacks in North Carolina perhaps enjoyed more legal rights than elsewhere in the South, their position began to erode in the 1820s. In 1827, the North Carolina legislature prohibited free blacks from immigrating to the state and directed county justices to seize "idle" free blacks and hire them out for up to three years. In response to David Walker's *Appeal,* the North Carolina legislature in 1830 made it a crime for free blacks to game with slaves or to teach slaves to read or write. Upon conviction, a free black could be fined, imprisoned, or whipped, at the discretion of the court. Free blacks were also prevented from selling any products outside their county of residence, and if they left the state for more than ninety days, they could not return. The legislature enacted a few additional restrictions on free blacks in 1831 in the wake of the Turner rebellion, but the "Free Black Code" was virtually complete by 1830. John Hope Franklin, *The Free Negro in North Carolina, 1790–1860* (Chapel Hill: University of North Carolina Press, 1943), 62–72.

21. In 1835 a North Carolina convention revised the state's constitution. Among other reforms, the convention revoked the right of free blacks to vote. A few representatives echoed the logic Kingsley employed in his support of the free black franchise by urging that the black vote be limited by property qualifications; this reform, they argued, would "retain the incentive value for enterprising free Negroes, while at the same time encouraging them to emulate the whites rather than their enslaved brethren." A proponent of disfranchisement, James W. Bryan, insisted that "North Carolina is the only Southern State . . . that has *permitted* them to enjoy this privilege; and so far as my experience and observation extends, her interests have not been promoted by the concession of the privilege." Harold J. Counihan, "The North Carolina Constitutional Convention of 1835: A Study in Jacksonian Democracy," *North Carolina Historical Review* 46 (October 1969): 346–48; Franklin, *The Free Negro in North Carolina,* 105–16.

3d. To extinguish that general foreign or northern prejudice against holding slave property, which commonly arises from their mistaken view of our policy and laws to regulate slaves and free colored people.

To accomplish these objects will require a considerable sacrifice of local prejudice to the shrine of self interest, with some small mixture of discretion, which I flatter myself the present enlightened state of society, improved by its advancement in the science of political economy, will, in consideration of the proposed advantages, liberally bestow. [Health and bodily perfection, are certainly before all other objects the most important; and to attain these, no sacrifice of any kind should be considered as too great. Improving the breed of domestic animals, has occupied the attention of some of the most eminent and useful men in our country. How much more meritorious and laudable would that philanthrophist be to whose energy and moral courage mankind were indebted for exposing and removing a prejudice that not only continues to entail ill health and degeneracy on the people, but completely neutralizes the physical strength of the country, by placing one portion of the inhabitants in hostile array against the other.[1828, 1829]

The red aborigines were in this low country a healthy people. The negroes are not only a healthy people, but robust and durable even in [the[1828, 1829]] swamps.

The intermediate grades of color are not only healthy, but when condition is favorable, they are [improved in shape, strength and beauty, and[1828, 1829]] susceptible of every amelioration. Daily experience shows that there is no natural antipathy between the castes on account of color; and it only requires to repeal laws as impolitic as they are unjust and unnatural; which confound [beauty,[1828, 1829]] merit, and condition [in one state of[1828, 1829]] [with[1833, 1834]] infamy and degradation on account of complexion, and to leave nature to find out a safe and wholesome remedy for evils which[, of all others, are now the most deplorable, because they are morally irreconcilable to the fundamental principles of happiness, and self preservation[1828, 1829]] [are merely imaginary[1833, 1834]] [, and unfit subjects for legislation[1834]].

[Appendix.

Since the year 1829, when the second edition of this pamphlet was published, the subject of our colored population has been pretty fully discussed in several of the State Legislatures of this Union, without arriving at any positive or satisfactory conclusion, as to how it would be safest and best to dispose of them, so as to avoid the risk of reaction from their resentment.

The alarm occasioned by the massacre at Southampton,[22] naturally caused a fear and diffidence in that quarter, which spread itself throughout the slave holding states, and operated with extreme cruelty and injustice against all the colored people, by confounding the innocent with the guilty;[23] and it is hardly a matter of doubt whether or not the excessive rigor and cruelty of these consequent enactments has not been very prejudicial to the slave holding interest, by causing a general feeling of compassion which is naturally excited in favor of helpless innocence, when oppressed by relentless tyranny. Colonization in Africa has been proposed to the free colored people, to forward which a general system of persecution against them, upheld from the pulpit, has been legalized throughout the southern states, which leaves them the sad alternative of submitting to a condition worse than slavery, or of leaving the country to which nativity has given them a

22. On the night of August 21, 1831, Nat Turner (1800–1831), a slave in Southampton County, Virginia, led other slaves in initiating the bloodiest slave rebellion in American history. Convinced early in life that God had chosen him for a divine purpose, Turner's thoughts turned increasingly apocalyptic when he became an adult. Other slaves, impressed by his intelligence and religious convictions, deemed him a prophet. Moving from plantation to plantation on August 21 and 22, the rebels killed fifty-five whites, mostly women and children, gathering supplies and recruits along the way. After two days of slaughter, the rebellion was crushed and most of the rebels were killed or captured. Turner eluded capture until October 30. He was tried early in November, convicted of "conspiring to rebel and make insurrection," and hanged on November 11. Stephen B. Oates, *The Fires of Jubilee: Nat Turner's Fierce Rebellion* (New York: Harper and Row, 1975). For primary documents see Henry I. Tragle, *The Southampton Slave Revolt of 1831: A Compilation of Source Material* (Amherst, Mass.: University of Massachusetts Press, 1971).

23. In the wake of Turner's rebellion, fears of similar slave uprisings ran rampant throughout the South. The Virginia House of Delegates debated emancipation as a solution but approved instead a more restrictive slave code. Other southern states likewise passed more restrictive legislation governing their black populations, free and slave, and previously existing laws were more strictly enforced. Although Turner was a slave, free people of color often bore the brunt of the legislative reaction to Turner's rebellion. Alabama, Maryland, and Tennessee prohibited free blacks from entering their borders; North Carolina, South Carolina, and Virginia had already passed such laws. Mississippi expelled free blacks between 16 and 50 years of age, unless they obtained a license of their "good character." Maryland and Virginia prohibited free blacks from possessing firearms. Because Turner was a preacher, free blacks and slaves were prohibited from preaching or assembling for religious services, except perhaps under strict supervision, in Mississippi, North Carolina, and Virginia. Fearing that unruly Virginia slaves were being exported to their state, several state legislatures in the Lower South prohibited the importation of slaves for sale. Herbert Aptheker, *Nat Turner's Slave Rebellion* (New York: Humanities Press, 1966), 74–94; Franklin, *The Free Negro in North Carolina,* 42–43; Alison Goodyear Freehling, *Drift Toward Dissolution: The Virginia Slavery Debate of 1831–1832* (Baton Rouge: Louisiana State University Press, 1982); Judith Kelleher Schafer, "The Immediate Impact of Nat Turner's Insurrection on New Orleans," *Louisiana History* 21 (fall 1980): 361–76.

natural right [, to go where sickness, privations and barbarity must soon put an end to all their troubles[1833]]; in this dilemma it is to be hoped that some way of escape will present itself.[24]

The same subject has excited an interest gradually proportioned to its magnitude, throughout all the American colonies, and has been regulated by acts of legislation dictated by circumstances connected with the views and prejudices of each.

The Swedish, Danish and French, have abolished the distinction of color where the parties are free, by admitting them to a participation of equal rights. The British have gone still further, and not only assimilated the interests of the free people of color of their colonies with those of the whites, but have threatened to extend their legislation to the emancipation of the slaves; this premature interference is generally condemned, as tending to overturn and destroy civilization, by too suddenly admitting an overwhelming proportion of ignorant and uncivilized people into society.

The Spanish colonies of Cuba and Puerto Rico have flourished beyond example without altering the wise, liberal, and humane policy of their former system, which protected the slaves from acts of cruelty and injustice, and at the same time united the interests of the free colored people to those of the whites, so as to form one consolidated mass of effective force under the complete control of their government.

Cuba, perhaps, under its present circumstances, stands more independent of external help, than any other slave holding government in America,

24. The American Colonization Society, organized in Washington, D.C., in 1816, established the colony of Liberia on the northwestern coast of Africa in 1822 as a refuge for free blacks and freed slaves from the United States. Unpopular with both abolitionists, who thought colonization strengthened slavery in the South, and northern blacks, who had no desire to leave their homeland for Africa, the colonization society declined after 1840. Some southern free blacks and freedpeople, hoping to begin a new life in Africa, did support the American Colonization Society. Between 1822 and 1860, more than 11,000 African Americans emigrated to Liberia. P. J. Staudenraus, *The African Colonization Movement, 1816–1865* (New York: Columbia University Press, 1961); Marie Tyler McGraw, "Richmond Free Blacks and African Colonization, 1816–1832," *Journal of American Studies* 21 (August 1987): 207–24. For the Liberian perspective, see Tom W. Schick, *Behold the Promised Land: A History of Afro-American Settler Society in Nineteenth-Century Liberia* (Baltimore, Md.: Johns Hopkins University Press, 1977), and Amos J. Beyan, *The American Colonization Society and the Creation of the Liberian State: A Historical Perspective, 1822–1900* (Lanham, Md.: University Press of America, 1991).

During the early years of settlement in Liberia, 22 percent of all immigrants died within one year of their arrival. Schick, *Behold the Promised Land*, 27–28; Tom W. Schick, "A Quantitative Analysis of Liberian Colonization from 1820 to 1843, with Special Reference to Mortality," *Journal of African History* 12 (1971): 45–59.

except Brazil. Its population may be estimated at one million, one third of which is free people, all united in the same interest; the other two thirds are slaves, who, being justly treated, have never manifested any signs of discontent.[25] Its soil is extremely fertile, its climate is healthy, its situation convenient for commerce, which it carries on with its own people, its export productions are immense, and its revenue competent for all the purposes of good government.

The empire of Brazil was left in a former edition of this work, at war with its neighbor, the republic [of[1834]] Buenos Ayres, which has since happily terminated, and proved the possibility of a country whose revenues and government depend entirely upon slave labor for support, being so entirely independent as not to require any foreign or external protection to enable it to resist a foreign enemy, without fear of a revolt from its own numerous slave population.[26] Since the termination of that war, several political convulsions and party revolutions [have[1833]] [had[1834]] happened within it; just enough to prove its stability, but there has been no sign or suspicion of any discontent among the slaves; and it now stands fairly and firmly upon its own national resources, and solely under its own protection, unparalleled in its extent, situation, and prospects of greatness derived from its healthy climate, fertility, and extent of territory, all convenient for commerce, which is extensively carried on by its own inhabitants, and protected by equitable and just laws. It now proudly and practically claims the only banner of actual independence belonging to any slave holding state in America.

Since that period, also, our own colored population, having been consolidated into one mass and identified with slavery by our state laws, has retrograded exceedingly in the southern states, without producing the desired effect of increasing the proportion of whites, and has proved incontestibly, I think, that the policy of persecuting the free colored people to induce them to sacrifice their native attachments and property for banish-

25. Slaves never comprised two-thirds of Cuba's population. In 1827, Cuba's total population of 704,487 consisted of 44 percent whites, 15 percent free people of color, and 40 percent slaves. Cohen and Greene, eds., *Neither Slave Nor Free*, 339.

26. The war ended in October 1828 when, through British diplomatic mediation, both Brazil and Argentina approved the independence of the Banda Oriental. In 1830 Brazil and Argentina accepted the constitution establishing the Republic of Uruguay as an independent buffer state. The war had been very unpopular in Brazil, especially because of military recruitment and the burden it placed on national finances. The unsuccessful war added to Brazilians' dissatisfaction with Emperor Dom Pedro I. In April 1831, he abdicated the Brazilian throne in favor of his five-year-old son. Seckinger, *The Brazilian Monarchy and the South American Republics*, 144–51; Leslie Bethell, ed., *Brazil: Empire and Republic, 1822–1930* (Cambridge: Cambridge University Press, 1989), 54, 57–58.

ment to Africa, is at variance with the prosperity and interests of the South, and tends to lower the price of property by destroying the prospect of its durability.

By persecution we force them off, and place them in a situation to retaliate upon us in case of war, and perhaps to glut their vengeance upon us at some future period, for no person can seriously believe that they are going to remain long in a savage and sterile country like Liberia, when so many healthy, fertile, and civilized countries, every where around, are inviting them to citizenship, and we well know that revenge for cruelty and injustice is a hereditary passion in human [nature[1833]] [heart[1834]]: handed down from father to son, it never dies until satiated by atonement.

As any argument about the justice and right of such laws can always be answered by the plea of expediency, it would be useless to enter into it farther than to observe that the policy of unjust laws is more than doubtful in any case whatever, especially as attended by the hostility naturally consequent to acts of cruelty and injustice, which must [necessarily[1833]] [naturally[1834]] produce resentment uncompensated for by any [subsequent[1833]] [probable[1834]] benefit. This could never have been fairly considered, or it never would have been attempted.

First, I will allow that it is physically possible to exterminate all the free colored people of the South, it makes no matter how; say about one hundredth part of all the free colored people of this quarter of the world is destroyed, the quantity of resentment of the remainder, and of all justly thinking men, will still be measured by the atrocity of the act.

Second. Will the same instinctive passion which caused their existence diminish, or will the same regular quantity of colored people still continue to be produced by that passion? If it will, destroying the present existing race will be playing the part of the Danaides in the story, attempting to fill the continually leaking pitcher;[27] besides, this system of tyranny and injus-

---

27. The Danaides in Greek mythology were the fifty daughters of King Danaus. Fearing his brother Aegyptus and Aegyptus's fifty sons, Danaus fled Egypt for Argos with his daughters. Argos had no water because of the wrath of Poseidon, who wanted Argos for himself though it had been allotted to Hera. Danaus sent his daughters in search of water, and Poseidon fell in love with one of them, Amymone, whom he showed the existence of a spring to provide water. Later, Danaus invited his fifty nephews to visit, and they announced their intentions of marrying his daughters. After a feast to celebrate the weddings, each of the Danaides followed her father's instructions and killed her husband, except the oldest, Hypermnestra, who spared her husband Lynceus. Later Lynceus killed the Danaides to avenge his brothers' deaths. The Danaides were punished in Hades by being compelled to refill leaking water-pots forever. Pierre Grimal, *The Dictionary of Classical Mythology*, trans. A. R. Maxwell-Hyslop (New York: Basil Blackwell, 1986), 40, 127.

tice is a libel upon our pretended republican institutions, incompatible with our national character, and cannot be considered but as an affront and open violation of the morality and civilization [of[1833]] [in[1834]] the age we live in. But what is still worse during its continuance, it evidently involves the necessary dependence of every individual slave holding state, upon foreign protection against itself. [To point out how it would be invidious,[1833]] no political association under the present laws against color could assure independence [of[1833]] [to[1834]] the slave holding states. The want of ordinary population would render regular white soldiers difficult to be got as well as expensive, and quite inefficient in the sickly season, when they might be most wanted. And the want of sailors would render commerce too expensive to be carried on amongst ourselves, and foreigners would carry away as they do now, all the profits of our labor; we therefore would be too poor to meet the expenses of such an exotic and unnatural independent government. Dependence therefore is our doom; we must seek protection from the free states who have a disposable population to make soldiers of, or to man ships to protect us, and to carry away our produce together with all the profits of our labor.

The consequences of some recent attempts at independence on the part of some slave holding states bring the above facts home to us; therefore to irritate that necessary and unoffending class of people by cruelty and injustice is impolitic, and completely defeats the object of our ever becoming independent.

The whole colored population of the United States, even including slaves, would not be more than one eighth part of those who immediately surround us; destroy them all, root and branch, they could easily be replaced at some future time; but until they were replaced, our southern seaboard country would offer a safe retreat for the bear and the wolf without competition.

Experiment is the fairest and most convincing argument; truth itself is only proved by connecting insulated facts; our mistaken system of policy has proved its fallacy by late events, and showed us that we are wrong; to persist in error is dangerous; let us take lessons from the laws of those countries which have already tested their policy by their beneficial effects with regard to slaves and free people of color, [and[1833]] who are all united and friendly to the interest of the whites, and to society generally; similar causes must produce similar effects; as we are the first in intelligence, so let us be first in the practice of political wisdom; and by uniting the interests of our whole population with that of our government, in support of national freedom and independence, rid ourselves of the most tormenting of all fears—that of ourselves.

Query. What would be the natural consequence of granting the same legal protection to the persons and properties of all free people alike, or the free use and benefit of the law to protect themselves?

Answer. They would all have the same means of acquiring property, and all would feel equally interested in the public welfare and peace of the country.

Query. Is the increase of free colored people injurious or beneficial to the seaboard country of the South?

Answer. In all the southern seaboard country which is unfavorable to the agricultural labors of white people, the increase of a free colored population is not only beneficial, but absolutely necessary, to its stability and to cheapen the price of labor, without which neither domestic commerce, nor mechanical operations, nor manufactures can be carried on to advantage, as is clearly demonstrated by the present state of poverty and dependence of that section, owing evidently to the want of cheap labor, which can only be obtained from a settled population attached to the soil.

Query. What national benefit is derived from the acts of outlawry now in force against the free colored people of the south?

Answer. No benefit whatever, but the greatest and most tormenting of all evils—a conscious dread of criminal guilt, arising from the known tyranny of the lawless and unprincipled part of the white population which the law authorises to perpetrate every species of wicked abuse upon innocence and unoffending color, which is entirely excluded from legal protection, except through the means of white evidence. Moral restraint without the fear of law being so rare, as to create a doubt whether or not the conscientious principle of justice, independent of legal restraint, has any real existence in the human breast.

Query. Has any property left by will to any colored person, ever been honestly and fairly administered by any white person?

Answer. Such instances might possibly have happened, but never to my knowledge.

Query. What must be the ultimate tendency of such a system of tyranny and injustice?

Answer. By exciting the indignation of the world, it must accelerate its own downfall. A government whose laws grant exclusive privileges to the wicked and abandoned part of its population, to persecute and destroy the weak of another humble part, is a government of anarchy; to call such a government a Republic, would be a gross libel on the name: it is ultra democracy or anarchy.

Query. What remedy could be proposed for this unsafe state of society?

Answer. Either to modify or repeal the most oppressive parts the laws now in force, or to improve the moral principles of the lower orders of white society by a more liberal education, such as would govern their actions by principles of moral justice, without the constraint of law; as the jealousy and injustice of the different grades of society, in their present conduct towards colored people seems to be graduated by the cultivation of their minds in moral economy, or the rule of conscientiously treating their fellow men justly, without regard to law, and just as they would like to be treated themselves, if placed under similar circumstances. Of the two remedies, the last would be the most radical and effectual, but being the most expensive and the most tedious, would come too late to remedy the present evils, which are now pressing upon society, and calling for immediate relief.[1833, 1834]]

Figure 1. Slave cabins, Kingsley Plantation, Fort George Island, Florida. Kingsley's slaves built thirty-two slave cabins of tabby—a mixture of lime, oyster shell, sand, and water—in a semicircular arc facing the plantation's main house. By permission of the P. K. Yonge Library of Florida History, University of Florida, Gainesville.

Figure 2. Main house, Kingsley Plantation, Fort George Island, Florida. Kingsley owned the island plantation from 1814 to 1839, and this house was his primary residence during most of his life in Florida. Courtesy of Jane F. Upton, photographer. By permission of the National Park Service, Timucuan Ecological and Historic Preserve, Jacksonville, Florida.

Figure 3. Kitchen house, Kingsley Plantation, Fort George Island, Florida. Courtesy of Jane F. Upton, photographer. By permission of the National Park Service, Timucuan Ecological and Historic Preserve, Jacksonville, Florida.

Notes.

(1) It will reasonably be inquired, who is the writer? and how presumes he to advise in contradiction to common practice and the received opinion of nine-tenths of all the slave owners of the United States? He answers that he is a slave owner, and has a right to express his opinion, having lived by planting in Florida for the last twenty-five years. He disavows all other motives but that of increasing the value of his property; moreover, he thinks that truth will support his arguments as to a subject with which he has had great opportunities of becoming well acquainted, having lived long in different slave holding countries.

(2) This observation will apply to many of our farmers whose youth, strength, and ambition seem for several years to set the climate at defiance, but they are finally overcome by sickness, which brings on debility and premature old age.

(3) Northern [migration[1828, 1829, 1833]] [emigration[1834]] to the south for the purpose of gain in winter, and southern [migration[1828, 1829, 1833]] [emigration[1834]] to the north to spend money in the summer, finally concentrate in the north the whole product of southern slave labor.

Slavery is a necessary state of control from which no condition of society can be perfectly free. The term is applicable to, and fits all grades and conditions in almost every point of view, whether moral, physical, or political.

It certainly is a mistaken notion that the progress of labor, guided by the accidental impulse of single individuals, is greater than that of systematic co-operation, directed and controlled by a skilful mechanic and economist, under the patriarchal government; for it is evident that slaves taught early, could produce any kind of manufactured goods one-third cheaper than free people; the co-operative system of labor being better calculated either to increase the quantity or to attain perfection in the manufacture; and whenever labor, expended in manufacturing cotton into cloth, yields more than it does when employed in raising the raw material, slaves will become manufacturers.[28]

(4) As white people are only wanted to act as overseers, or to fill vacancies in conformity to law, their number must always be limited to these wants and easy situations. But the number of colored people must eventually be bounded by the quantity, and quality of soil from which they derive subsistence by manual labor.

28. For a discussion of slaves in manufacturing and industrial employment, see Robert S. Starobin, *Industrial Slavery in the Old South* (New York: Oxford University Press, 1970).

(5) Pride and prejudice, our present stumbling blocks in the management of our negroes, should give way to policy and the necessity of self preservation, and induce us to remove as far as possible whatever are the obvious causes of this dangerous spirit of revolt.

Power may for a while triumph over weakness and misfortune. But as all nature (from the eternal principle of self) takes part with weakness against power, the re-action finally must be terrible and overwhelming.

(6) Whoever was so unlucky as to see, on Cumberland Island, last war, the magical transformation of his own negroes, whom he left in the field but a few hours before, into regular soldiers, of good discipline and appearance, and with what despatch and celerity the recruiting service went on under the protection of a few hundred marines, notwithstanding all the care and vigilence that [was[1828, 1829]] [were[1833, 1834]] used to prevent desertion, could not help figuring to himself the consequences had there been a larger force, able to maintain a position on the main, with any ulterior object of conquest in view, and possessing the means of equipment. Where would they have stopped, or what could have stopped them?[29]

(7) The empire of Brazil embraces, from north to south, about one thousand leagues of sea coast, and as many from east to west. The whole of this immense territory[, in[1828, 1829]] [is[1833, 1834]] a wholesome, temperate, and warm climate, is watered by the largest and most extensive rivers in the world, and possesses abundance of capacious and deep harbours for shipping, with inexhaustible quantities of incorruptible timber, of which it has already built some of the finest first-rate ships of war and merchantmen that any country can boast of. Its export agricultural produce is fast approaching in value to that of the United States, and it is incontestably the most extensive, [valuable[1828, 1829]] [valued[1833, 1834]], rich, healthy, and best situated body of land under any one government in America; and bids fair, from its policy and form of government, which is a limited monarchy, to be one of the most durable. Its present population, being more than three-fourths colored, will

29. During the War of 1812, Admiral Sir George Cockburn of the British navy seized Cumberland Island, the southernmost sea island on the Georgia coast, and held it from January to March 1815. The British presence on Cumberland Island and their promises of freedom drew slaves from the surrounding area in Georgia and Spanish East Florida. As many as 1,483 slaves made their way to British ships; only 81 were returned to Cumberland Island slave owners when the Treaty of Ghent ended the war and the British departed. The Georgia legislature, at its next session in November 1815, enacted harsher laws against free blacks. The legislature began the process, completed in 1841, of closing off the possibility of manumission. In 1816 the Georgia legislature condemned to be sold into slavery for life any free black convicted of enticing slaves away from their owners. Mary R. Bullard, *Black Liberation on Cumberland Island in 1815* (DeLeon Springs, Fla.: E. O. Painter, 1983).

rapidly predominate on that side, on account of its convenient situation to Africa, its immense annual importation of slaves, its rich soil, its temperate and healthy climate, and more especially from its great distance, and the expense of passages from Europe. With Chinese economy it may, at some period not very remote, compete in population with that most ancient Empire, which it greatly exceeds in extent. Of all other countries, in fact, it most resembles China in its climate, fertility of soil, and complexion of inhabitants.

(8) I heard of no instance of abuse or treachery on the part of the negroes of Grand Anse, during my residence in Jeremie, while it was held by the British; nor did I experience either insult or interruption in the south or west of St. Domingo, under the government of Touissant, or Rigaud. I resided there nearly a year, at one period, besides making frequent voyages, during which I often travelled alone, and on horseback, from Leogane to the Cayes, and from Petit-Goave to Jacquemel, through woods and over mountains, with my saddle bags loaded with specie to buy coffee; and though I frequently met large groups of armed negroes in the woods, I neither received insult or hinderance, but was always treated with kindness and civility. Many Americans, (I may say hundreds) at that time on the Island, can testify to the same treatment and circumstances.[30]

(9) This observation applies only to neutral nations. The French, who were at war and enemies, were several times not only plundered but killed within the government of Rigaud: but under Touissant, I knew of no instance of treachery, and all nations, classes, and conditions were equally protected.

(10) For the truth of this observation, I appeal to every slave holder in the south, who has had an opportunity of witnessing the conduct of white laborers who come annually to seek work from the north; whether the common plantation negroes do not conduct themselves much better and are of a more respectable moral character.

(11) Our laws to regulate slaves are entirely founded on terror. It would be worthwhile to try the experiment of a small mixture of reward with the punishment—such as allowing them the free use of Sunday as a market day and jubilee, which I have observed had a good effect in all foreign countries, also in Louisiana. The laws of the southern states are exclusively con-

30. Petit Goâve and Léogane were cities on the northern coast of the southern peninsula of Saint Domingue; Les Cayes and Jacmel were cities on the southern coast of the same peninsula. The British held the Grand' Anse portion of the peninsula from 1793 to 1798 and Léogane for a portion of that time. Much of the rest of the region was under the Republican control of André Rigaud.

structed for the protection of whites, and vexatious tyranny over the persons and properties of every colored person, whose oath can in no case be admitted as evidence against a white person. Policy and self-preservation require, to render the [co-operative[1828, 1829]] system beneficial, that slaves must be kept under wholesome and just restraint, which must always create some degree of resistance more or less to Patriarchal authority; to counterbalance which the interest and co-operation of the free colored people is absolutely necessary when the white population is scanty.

(12) A slave who saves my life by rescuing it from assassins at the risk of his own; or who saves the lives and properties of a whole community by informing against conspirators must still remain a slave! and what a dreadful feeling of general resentment must originate from such a source of injustice! [No wonder (with such laws) at the universal antipathy and detestation against slavery, thus identified with tyranny and the most oppressive cruelty.[1828, 1829]]

(13) What greater insult can be offered to common sense, than to arrogate the condition of freedom to ourselves, who have not the power, under any circumstances, of disposing of our property in the way we please. Is there any thing worthy of acceptance that can be offered to a slave but freedom? [And that we have not within our gift in many of our States.[1828, 1829]][31]

If our low country is destroyed, and I lose my life and property by an insurrection, what satisfaction is it to me to know that our back country militia will promptly and bravely revenge my death and destroy my negroes? A state of war might soon produce such an event.

A very common argument against free colored people's testimony being admitted as evidence in all cases is, that their moral character is not generally so respectable. The force of all testimony must be measured by its respectability; therefore of unequal value. But that the moral character of free colored people generally, is inferior to that of the same condition of

31. Some southern states—Alabama, Georgia, Mississippi, and South Carolina—allowed manumission only by an act of the state legislature. Several states—Alabama, Maryland, North Carolina, Tennessee, and Virginia—required that emancipated blacks leave the state. Provisions for manumission tightened considerably in the 1850s, with many states forbidding the practice entirely. Florida's first Legislative Council in 1822 passed a law allowing emancipation, which was continued when that act was superseded by legislation in 1824. In 1829 the Legislative Council passed "An Act to Prevent the Manumission of Slaves, in Certain Cases, in this Territory," which sharply restricted manumission by forcing owners to pay $200 for every slave manumitted and the freed person to leave the Territory within thirty days. Berlin, *Slaves Without Masters*, 138–39; *Acts of the Legislative Council of the Territory of Florida, 1822*, 183–84; *Acts of the Legislative Council of the Territory of Florida, 1824*, 289–90; *Acts of the Legislative Council of the Territory of Florida, 1829*, 134–35.

whites, I think cannot be proved. On the contrary, all unprejudiced people who have had an opportunity of knowing, and have paid attention to the subject, will say that the very opposite is the case. Even if it were not so, what a reflection on our policy and justice, to outlaw them for complexion, which they cannot help, and deprive them of the means of acquiring moral improvement, by driving them to seek shelter among the slaves! Few, I think, will deny that color and condition, if properly considered, are two very separate qualities. But the fact is, that in almost every instance, our legislators, for want of due consideration, have mistaken the shadow for the substance, and confounded together two very different things; thereby substantiating by law a dangerous and inconvenient antipathy, which can have no better foundation than prejudice. It is much to be regretted that those who enact laws to regulate slaves, and free people of color, are often obliged to consult popularity rather than policy and their own good sense. If such alterations were practicable as would render slave property safe, without adopting the present system of terror, all such laws as tended to regulate plantation management, and interfere with the province of individual owners, could be repealed; property would increase in value; and the owner, no longer a kind of state prisoner, hovering over the movements of his negroes and overseers, could liberalize and improve his mind by travelling, and satisfy his thirst for knowledge wherever the advance of science offered the greatest field for its acquirement.

The patrol laws are demoralizing to the whites who compose the patrol; tyrannical and unjust to the negroes; and unnecessarily supercede, in most cases, the owner's prerogative and rights over his property.

Some of our state laws, in defiance of our national treaties, condemn to indiscriminate imprisonment in the common jail, every class of free colored persons, who may arrive within their limits, without reference to sex, cause, or condition; and to be sold as slaves where they have not the means of paying the penalties annexed to the crime of arriving within the jurisdiction of the law. What must be the final consequence of such infatuation? an infatuation arraying itself in open and avowed hostility against [twelve[1828, 1829, 1833]] [twenty[1834]] millions of people, now composing the colored population of this quarter of the world. Hayti, alone, in the full career of wealth, freedom, and juvenile independence, with equal, if not superior, advantages of climate, soil, and situation, to any equal portion of territory in the world, [and[1828, 1829]] [is[1833, 1834]] evidently destined by nature, at no very distant period, if not to command, at least to share the commerce of the surrounding ocean; and, without being over peopled, comfortably to accommodate twelve millions of inhabitants.

A war of color would, in our situation, of all wars be the most dangerous; therefore the least advisable, because we naturally and unavoidably (under our present policy) contain within us the materials of our own dissolution; and nine-tenths of all our present white friends would at least laugh at our absurd indiscretion.

All the late insurrections of slaves are to be traced to [influential[1828, 1829]] [fanatical[1833, 1834]] preachers [of the gospel,[1828, 1829]] (as, for instance, at Barbadoes[32] and Demarara,[33]) [and[1833, 1834]] to white [preachers,[1828, 1829]] (missionaries) from England.[34] Vesey, who instigated the Charleston plot,

32. On Easter Sunday in 1816, several thousand of the 77,000 slaves on the British sugar-producing island of Barbados rose in rebellion. Slaves on at least seventy plantations had started fires and seized weapons. British regulars and black militia quelled the revolt in a matter of days. Only one white man and one black militiaman were killed; at least fifty slaves died in the fighting and another seventy were summarily executed on the field. Some 300 more slaves and a handful of free blacks were tried, 144 of whom were executed and another 132 were deported. Free blacks comprised only 3 percent of the Barbadian population, but "the free colored class was a cause of social unrest rather than the buffer it might have been." Most free blacks were lost between the white and slave population, but a "significant few . . . felt a greater social and racial affinity with the slave majority." Some of this latter group became leaders in the 1816 rebellion. Michael Craton, *Testing the Chains: Resistance to Slavery in the British West Indies* (Ithaca, N.Y.: Cornell University Press, 1982), 254–66; Jerome S. Handler, *The Unappropriated People: Freedom in the Slave Society of Barbados* (Baltimore, Md.: Johns Hopkins University Press, 1974).

33. In 1823, between 10,000 and 12,000 slaves revolted in the British colony of Demerara, an area on the northern coast of South America that later became a portion of Guyana. The suppression of the rebellion was quick and brutal, leaving two hundred slaves dead. Others were tried, and some of them were hanged. John Smith, a white evangelical missionary who had come from Britain in 1817 to preach to the slaves, was accused of instigating the rebellion. He too was tried and sentenced to death, though the young preacher died in jail awaiting the outcome of an appeal. Emilia Viotti da Costa, *Crowns of Glory, Tears of Blood: The Demerara Slave Rebellion of 1823* (New York: Oxford University Press, 1994); Craton, *Testing the Chains,* 267–90.

34. Eugene Genovese notes that black drivers, artisans, and preachers often provided the leadership for slave rebellions. These elite slaves or free blacks either "identify with their oppressors and seek individual advancement or they identify with their people and place their sophistication at the disposal of the rebellion. They thus produce a high percentage of leaders and traitors." Eugene Genovese, *From Rebellion to Revolution: Afro-American Slave Revolts in the Making of the Modern World* (Baton Rouge, La.: Louisiana State University Press, 1979), 28.

Curiously, Kingsley did not add the slave rebellion in Jamaica in 1831–32 to the third and fourth editions of his *Treatise,* which would seem to support his point. This largest and most widespread of all British West Indian slave uprisings involved 60,000 slaves, and some contemporaries attributed the "Baptist War" to the influence of Baptist missionaries among the slaves. Michael Craton, *Testing the Chains,* 291–321; Mary Turner, *Slaves and Missionaries: The Disintegration of Jamaican Slave Society, 1787–1834* (Urbana: University of Illinois Press, 1982), 148–73.

was an exhorting brother.[35] [What regret need it give to a slave, an orthodox believer, to know that he is going to die, or be removed from under the power of a wicked master, and miserable state of penance and oppression in an unhappy world, where he has been unjustly held in bondage, and placed in a state of misery by a beneficent and just being, to prepare him for a happy world hereafter, which is promised to all sinners who repent and are true believers; where he is to have plenty of every thing that is good and pleasant, without work or master; but if he does not believe in whatever is told him, he must be eternally tormented with fire and brimstone. To refuse the offer of such an alternative would prove any one to be either a fool or an unbeliever.[1828]] [Gullah Jack or Jack the Conjurer[36] was a [priest[1829]] [Conjurer[1833, 1834]] in his own country, M'Choolay Moreema, where a dialect of the Angola tongue is spoken clear across Africa from sea to sea, a distance perhaps of three thousand miles: I purchased him a prisoner of war at Zinguebar. He had his conjuring implements with him in a bag which he brought onboard the ship and always retained them.[1829, 1833, 1834]] I know [of[1828]] two instances, to the southward, where gangs of negroes were prevented from deserting to the enemy by drivers, or influential negroes, whose

35. Denmark Vesey (1767?-1822) was born a slave but purchased his freedom in 1800 and became a successful craftsman in Charleston, South Carolina. He became a class leader in the African Church of Charleston, formed in 1818 when most of the city's 6,000 African-American Methodists left the biracial Methodist Church. Uneasy over this expression of black autonomy, Charleston authorities closed the church in 1821. Convinced that slavery was contrary to God's will, angered by the closing of the African Church, and inspired by the example of the rebellion in Santo Domingo, Vesey gathered a group of followers from among Charleston's slave community. On July 14, 1822, they planned to raid the city arsenal and set fire to the city. Betrayed by other African Americans, both slave and free, Vesey and dozens of others were arrested. Vesey and thirty-four others were executed for plotting rebellion. In response to Vesey's abortive plot, the South Carolina legislature in 1822 sharply restricted the autonomy of free blacks. John Lofton, *Insurrection in South Carolina: The Turbulent World of Denmark Vesey* (Yellow Springs, Ohio: Antioch Press, 1964); Robert S. Starobin, ed., *Denmark Vesey: The Slave Conspiracy of 1822* (Englewood Cliffs, N.J.: Prentice-Hall, 1970); Michael P. Johnson and James L. Roark, *Black Masters: A Free Family of Color in the Old South* (New York: W. W. Norton, 1984), 37–43. For documents, see Lionel H. Kennedy and Thomas Parker, *An Official Report of the Trials of Sundry Negroes, Charged with an Attempt to Raise an Insurrection in the State of South Carolina* (Charleston, S.C., 1822) and John Oliver Killens, ed., *The Trial Record of Denmark Vesey* (Boston, Mass.: Beacon, 1970).

36. Gullah Jack Pritchard, an Angolan, was simultaneously a member of the African Methodist Church and a conjurer. He "empowered parched corn, ground nuts, and crab claws to protect those who joined the revolution." Other conspirators referred to him as "the little man who can't be killed, shot or taken." Johnson and Roark, *Black Masters*, 39; Albert J. Raboteau, *Slave Religion: The "Invisible Institution" in the Antebellum South* (New York: Oxford University Press, 1978), 163; Genovese, *From Rebellion to Revolution*, 46–47. For the compatibility of Christianity and conjure, see Raboteau, *Slave Religion*, 275–88.

integrity to their masters, and influence over the slaves prevented it; and what is still more remarkable, in both instances the influential negroes were Africans, and professors of the Mahomedan religion.[37]

A favorite maxim with some of our old southern politicians to increase the security of slave property has been to prohibit the increase of free people, or, by some means or other not yet divulged, to get rid of the evil altogether. If this could be done without making the remedy worse than the disease, it would be worth while to try it, but as the iniquity has its origin in a great [inherent[1828, 1829]] [instinctive[1833, 1834]], universal, and immutable law of nature, legislation, by the aged, against such an alleged crime as propagation in youth, would be hopeless, and like the story of the King of Arabia, who, after destroying his appetite by excess and gluttony, made a law forbidding, under a severe penalty, that any of his subjects should be hungry.

About twenty-five years ago, I settled a plantation on St. Johns River, in Florida, with about fifty new African negroes, many of whom I brought from the coast myself. They were mostly fine young men and women, and nearly in equal numbers. I never interfered with their connubial concerns, nor domestic affairs, but let them regulate these after their own manner. I taught them nothing but what was useful, and what I thought would add to their physical and moral happiness. I encouraged as much as possible dancing, merriment, and dress, for which Saturday afternoon and night, and Sunday morning were dedicated; and, after allowance, their time was usually employed in hoeing their corn, and getting a supply of fish for the week. Both men and women were very industrious. Many of them made twenty bushels of corn to sell, and they vied with each other in dress and dancing, and as to whose [woman[1828, 1829]] [wife[1833, 1834]] was the finest and prettiest. They were perfectly honest, and obedient, and appeared quite happy, having no fear but that of offending me; and I hardly ever had occasion to apply other correction than shaming them. If I exceeded this, the punishment was quite light, for they hardly ever failed in doing their work well. My object was to excite their ambition and attachment by kindness; not to depress their spirits by fear and punishment. I never allowed them to visit, for fear of bad example, but encouraged the decent neighboring people to participate in their weekly festivity, for which they always provided an ample

---

37. Eugene Genovese notes that "in the Caribbean and South America, religious leaders . . . led, inspired, or provided vital sanction for one revolt after another." Although Islam was not intrinsically more revolutionary than various forms of Christianity, "throughout the Americas, Muslim slaves earned a reputation for being especially rebellious. The political-religious ideology they brought from West Africa ill-prepared them for enslavement to infidels, whose power they were expected to resist." Genovese, *From Rebellion to Revolution*, 28–29.

entertainment themselves, as they had an abundance of hogs, fowls, corn, and all kinds of vegetables and fruit. They had nothing to conceal from me, and I had no suspicion of any crime in them to guard against. Perfect confidence, friendship, and good understanding reigned between us; they increased rapidly. After a few years, this pleasant and profitable state of harmony was interrupted by the revolution of 1812. A war party of Seminole Indians attacked the plantation in my absence; caught, bound, and carried off, or killed, forty of them, whose reluctance in going with the invaders may be imagined from the following circumstance. The wife of a young man they had tied and were driving off, that her husband, who was too strong to be handled, and who had his young child in his arms, might follow; but this he absolutely refused, handing over the child to his wife, and saying that she knew best how to take care of it, but that his master should never say that he was a runaway negro; upon which the Indian shot him, and he died next day.[38]

But my object in this long digression is to show the danger and hurtful tendency of superstition (by some called religion) among negroes, whose ignorance and want of rationality rendered them fit subjects to work upon. I afterwards purchased more new negroes. A man, calling himself a minister, got among them.[39] It was now sinful to dance, work their corn, or catch fish, on a Sunday; or to eat cat fish, because they had no scales; and if they did,

38. Between 1812 and 1815, some American settlers in the northern portion of East Florida attempted to establish a Republic of East Florida, independent of Spanish rule, which would petition for annexation by the United States. Although initially the Patriot Rebellion enjoyed some success, promised American support failed, and the Spanish reestablished their authority in the area. In the general upheaval caused by the rebellion, Seminole Indians attacked Kingsley's plantation on the St. Johns River and killed or abducted several of his slaves. Patrick, *Florida Fiasco*; *East Florida Claims: Case of Zephaniah Kingsley* (n.p., n.d.).

39. In July 1815 in the Mosquitos area south of St. Augustine, Robert McHardy brought charges against a free black Methodist preacher named Antonio Williams. McHardy insisted that Williams was "highly detrimental to the calmness and tranquility that the slaves should have" because he was "instilling them with depraved doctrines, which distracts them from good customs and which can occasion harmful consequences." Witnesses attributed the flight of many of the slaves in the area to Williams's preaching. Although uncertain what he preached, one witness was sure that "it cannot be a good thing when it is seen that said slaves are distracted from their duties, and the flight of many of them to the Indian nations has been suffered." After Williams was arrested, Governor Juan José de Estrada ordered that he be placed in solitary confinement in the Castillo de San Marcos in St. Augustine. Williams testified that he was sixty-seven years old, a cooper, and a native of Charleston. He denied the charges against him and implicated a slave preacher named Antonio (or Tony). Without further proceedings, the court determined that Williams should be expelled from East Florida and that the owner of the slave Tony should sell him outside of the province. East Florida Papers, Reel 126, Bundle 29001, Document 1815–4, Library of Congress, Washington, D.C.

they were to go to a place where they would be tormented with fire and brimstone to all eternity! They became poor, ragged, hungry, and disconsolate: to steal from me was only to do justice—to take what belonged to them because I kept them in unjust bondage; that all pastime or pleasure in this iniquitous world was sinful; that this was only a place of sorrow and repentance, and the sooner they were out of it the better; that they would then go to a good country, where they would experience no want of any thing, and have no work nor cruel taskmaster, for that God was merciful, and would pardon any sin they committed; only it was necessary to pray and ask forgiveness, and have prayer meetings, and contribute what they could to the church, &c.

They accordingly formed private societies under church regulations, where all were brothers and sisters, and, under an oath of the most horrid penalty, never to tell or divulge any crime that would bring any brother or sister into trouble, but to lay all the blame on those who had not united with them, and who, of necessity, were obliged to join the fraternity, as soon as possible, in their own defence. They had private nightly meetings, once or twice a week, with abundance of preaching and praying, (for they all exhorted, men as well as women) with an ample entertainment from my hogs, [as[1828, 1829]] [for[1833, 1834]] it was no sin to steal for the church, the elders of which held it right to break open my corn house, and provide amply for the meeting; so that, finally, myself and the overseer became completely divested of all authority over the negroes. The latter even went so far as to consult the head men of the church whether or not, according to religion, my orders ought to be obeyed! Severity had no effect; it only made it worse; and I really believe that, in several instances, sick children were allowed to die, because the parents thought conscientiously that it was meritorious to transfer their offspring from a miserable and wicked world to a happy country, where they were in hopes of soon joining them!

I relate the above circumstance not from any disrespect or [sectarian[1828]] prejudice against any particular religious profession; but when it renders men unhappy and discontented with their condition in life, by destroying local attachment and love of country, it certainly should be rationally opposed; and I cannot help regretting that honest, well meaning men, with so much ability to do good, and render mankind, especially the lower orders, happy and contented, should so misapply their talents as to subvert all natural and rational happiness, and endeavor to render our species miserable.

I was informed by a gentleman who lived near the Fishdam ford, on Broad River, South Carolina, that his employer had made an experiment

[in[1828]] [on[1829, 1833, 1834]] the management of negroes, of whom he was overseer, which answered extremely well, and offers to us a strong case in favor
of exciting ambition by cultivating utility, local attachment, and moral improvement, among slaves. He established four or five plantations, not far
apart, and stocked each of them with a suitable proportion of hands, and
work cattle, under a driver, who had the entire management of every thing
under his (the overseer's) control. The overseer's duty merely extended to
direct[ing[1828]] the driver on what land he was to raise provisions, and where
cotton was to be planted; with this understanding, that all the cotton raised,
after it was cleaned and packed, belonged to the owner, and that all the
hogs, corn, and provisions left after supplying the plantation, belonged to
the negroes, who might do with it as they pleased.

The consequence of this arrangement was, that these plantations, regulated as before stated, turned out better crops than any other plantations of
equal force in that neighborhood, and the owner had no farther trouble nor
expense than furnishing the ordinary clothing and paying the overseer's
wages, so that he could fairly be called free, seeing that he could realize his
annual income wherever he chose to reside, without paying the customary
homage to servitude of personal attendance on the operations of his slaves.

Good policy requires that all laws tending to demoralize the people by
holding out a premium for perjury, should be abolished. [In 1828, a law was
passed at Tallahassie making the most virtuous, beautiful, or respectable
colored female liable to receive publicly on her bare back 39 lashes, on
conviction (of abusive language to any white person) before a justice of
peace, on the testimony of the most profligate white person.[1828]][40] Motives
of policy, self-preservation or justice, on which [the[1828]] laws [of the feeble
States, more especially such as Florida,[1828]] should be founded, form little or
no part in such laws, as far as regards the free colored people of the South,
(with some exceptions, such as North Carolina and Louisiana,) which are
dictated in a spirit of intolerant prejudice and irresponsible autocracy, holding out to people they nickname free, no positive reward or premium whatever for being virtuous; nothing to stimulate to industry or the acquisition
of a good name, learning, or refinement; no kind of protection either for

40. The law to which Kingsley here referred is Section 22 of the "Act Relating to Crimes and
Misdemeanors Committed by Slaves, Free Negroes and Mulattoes." This section provided
"That if any negro or mulatto, bond or free, shall at any time use abusive and provoking
language to, or lift his hand in opposition to any person not being a negro or mulatto, he, she
or they so offending shall for every such offense, proved by the oath of the party before a justice
of the peace . . . receive not exceeding thirty nine lashes on his or her bare back." *Acts of the
Legislative Council of the Territory of Florida, 1828,* 180.

person or property; their destiny is already fixed by a mark of nature which has doomed to irrevocable disgrace its degraded bearer, who is singled out as a victim for cruelty, avarice, and revenge; whose punishment must be corporeal, not even excepting the most delicate female, whose industry and virtue alone would place [her[1833, 1834]] at the head of society in any other country. The fruits of their industry must be offered up as a temptation to the avarice of some nobler color, which alone is privileged to hold and protect it. In short, liberty is merely nominal, without any constitutional protection. They may be sold for debt to pay partial, exorbitant, and tyrannical taxes or fines, all [of[1833, 1834]] which are unconstitutional. Oppression is carried to its greatest extreme when a mother of the most unexceptionable moral character, leaving her family on account of ill health, and going out of her native state, is inexorably punished by perpetual banishment from her husband, children, friends, country, and all that is dear to her.

Since these severe enactments against color, several of the most respectable and enterprising young men have withdrawn from their native country and entered into the Haytian navy, and more will undoubtedly follow. I should think it were better to induce such to remain at home as friends, than oblige them to pass the Rubicon as enemies.

It has been a favorite project of some of our least mathematical economists, to transport all the colored people of the U. States to Africa, without considering that the cost of the annual increase alone, if purchased, when added to the lowest possible freight, would exceed the annual revenue of the U[nited[1833, 1834]]. States.[41] Besides, the difficulty and stern opposition that would encounter a prostration of all rights of property and liberty of person, they would have to be put on board in irons, under a strong guard, and

41. American Colonization Society president Bushrod Washington frequently announced that a donation or public expenditure of $25 would fund the transportation of one free African American to Liberia. If Washington's estimate were correct, the federal government could have transported 1,200,000 blacks to Africa for the same amount spent on quelling Native American resistance in the Second Seminole War. Douglas R. Egerton, "Averting a Crisis: The Proslavery Critique of the American Colonization Society," *Civil War History* 43 (June 1997): 153.

In 1919, Early Lee Fox estimated that the American Colonization Society transported 1,430 emigrants to Liberia between 1820 and 1830. The society's expenditures during the same period were $106,367.72. Thus, Fox argues, the cost per emigrant was $74.38. Early Lee Fox, *The American Colonization Society, 1817–1840* (Baltimore, Md.: Johns Hopkins University Press, 1919), 88.

In contrast, Benjamin Lundy in 1825 estimated that 50,000 freed slaves could be sent to Haiti each year for $720,000, or a cost of $14.40 per emigrant. The actual costs per emigrant for the limited migration to Haiti that did take place in the 1820s and 1830s remain unknown. Dillon, *Benjamin Lundy,* 92.

be conveyed and landed with the same military formality, to oppose the resentment of the natives whom they must displace, as well as the vengeance of the convicts themselves, both of whose lives must be sacrificed to famine or resentment at the despotic nod of cruelty and superstition.

A great opportunity was lost of colonizing more rationally at the late evacuation of the Spanish part of Saint Domingo, where there would have been ample room for all the colored people of the U. States, within five days sail of Charleston.[42]

A patriarchal feeling of affection is due to every slave from his owner, who should consider the slave as a member of his family, whose happiness and protection is identified with that of his own family, of which his slave constitutes a part, according to his scale of condition. This affection creates confidence which becomes reciprocal, and is attended with the most beneficial consequences to both. It certainly is humiliating to a proud master to reflect, that he depends on his slave[s[1828]] even for bread to eat. But such is the fact.

In most foreign colonies where spring is perpetual, Saturday is allowed the slaves as a compensation for their furnishing their own provision, which chiefly consists of yams and plantains, produced almost spontaneously, or with little labor, and abundance of sweet, nutritious, and farinacious fruits of exquisite flavor, growing wild on the trees all the year round. This not only supplies them with delicious and wholesome food, but furnishes the means of traffic in the towns at night, or to carry to market on Sunday, which is every where celebrated as a day of freedom and rejoicing, similar to the practice at New Orleans.

Let any slave owner reflect and say how much advantage the country would derive from preaching up industry, economy, and a local attachment to the slaves; and, by pointing out to them the happy coincidence and wise and beneficent dispensation of so much good which every where surrounds them, how much he would be deserving of universal respect and gratitude;

---

42. The 1795 Treaty of Basle ended hostilities between France and Spain. In the treaty, the Spanish also ceded Santo Domingo, the Spanish colony consisting of the eastern two-thirds of the island of Haiti, to the French. However, in 1808–9, inhabitants of Santo Domingo revolted and restored Spanish rule. Capitalizing on weakening Spanish control, Haitian president Jean Pierre Boyer again took control of Santo Domingo in 1822 and united the island.

Between 1823 and 1826, Boyer oversaw the redistribution of land in the eastern two-thirds of the island from the church and large landowners to the freedpeople and small farmers. Boyer's land policies made him unpopular among the landowning residents of the former Santo Domingo, and opposition forced Boyer to end the policy in 1826.

instead of preaching up terror and dismay, misery and discontent, as dispensations of the supreme Author of all good. All local attachment and love of virtue must be chilled or annihilated by such intemperate abuse of supreme wisdom. Any extreme is said naturally to produce its opposite. Will an excess of error ever produce truth?

Circular in the *Working Man's Advocate*
(New York, 1831)[1]

For the Working Man's Advocate.[2]
Prejudice Against Color (*Circular.*)

1. Printed Letter. [Zephaniah or George Kingsley], "Prejudice Against Color," *Working Man's Advocate* (New York), October 1, 1831.
   The content and language of the circular suggests either that Zephaniah Kingsley wrote it or that he heavily influenced its content. If Zephaniah Kingsley did not write the circular, George Kingsley, his mulatto son, then twenty-four years old, was likely its author. In 1836, George Kingsley led his father's colonizing effort in Haiti; in 1831, the Kingsleys were considering Mexico as a suitable location to begin life anew away from Florida's harsh racial policies.
   2. George H. Evans established the *Working Man's Advocate* in New York City in 1829 as an organ of the Working Men, disgruntled and radical Jacksonian Democrats who felt abandoned by the Democratic political leadership. Early an advocate of educational reform, the *Working Man's Advocate* directed popular attention to economic inequalities between economic elites and the working classes. In 1835, Evans moved the *Working Man's Advocate* to Rahway, New Jersey, about thirty miles from Manhattan. In 1836, "citing exhaustion and poor health," Evans suspended publication of the newspaper. Evans revived the *Working Man's Advocate* in the mid-1840s to advocate again the cause of journeymen and artisans. Sean Wilentz, *Chants Democratic: New York City and the Rise of the American Working Class, 1788–1850* (New York: Oxford University Press, 1984), 197, 240, 336, 341.
   In one of its first issues, the *Working Man's Advocate* published a notice from the firm of Lundy and Garrison in Baltimore "to humane, conscientious Slaveholders" asking for slaves "to remove and settle in the Republic of Hayti, where they will be forthwith invested with the rights of freemen, and receive constant employment, and liberal wages, in a healthy and pleasant section of the country." The notice asked all newspapers "friendly to the colonization of the colored race" to reprint it. "Emigration to Hayti," *Working Man's Advocate*, December 12, 1829.
   Benjamin Lundy (1789–1839) began the publication in Ohio in 1821 of a newspaper titled *Genius of Universal Emancipation*, which was devoted to the eradication of slavery. By 1829, Lundy and new partner William Lloyd Garrison published the newspaper in Baltimore. Through the 1820s, Lundy supported the colonization of freed blacks in Haiti though he did not share others' racist desire to rid the United States of all free blacks. Lundy eventually turned from Haiti to Mexico as the solution to finding a site for African-American emigration. In 1831, Lundy, like Kingsley, rejected Canada and promoted the idea of emigration to the Mexican province of Texas. Dillon, *Benjamin Lundy,* 144–46, 165–69.

The history of the world in the present and past ages, proves that jealousy and prejudice are the offspring of ignorance or want of liberal education; therefore, the liberality and justice of the laws of any country may be considered as a standard measure by which the comparative state of civilization of that country may be fairly estimated. The truth of this proposition has of late been appreciated and partially applied to practice by those among our State Governments which are farthest advanced in civilization; and no doubt but that others will eventually adopt the same enlightened course of improvement; so all schools and seminaries of instruction throughout the Union will have but one object in view: viz. the teaching of human wisdom and happiness; and but one effect in practice, viz. to produce national stability founded on a true and just estimate of the economy of action required to produce rational happiness; or, in fewer words, the cultivation and maturing of our rational faculties.

Whether a sufficient quantity of this rational principle will be cultivated and obtain circulation throughout the Union in time to prevent the worst evils springing from ignorance, viz. discord and the rule of the strongest, is a problem yet to be solved.

I think, however, it will be universally conceded, that to perpetuate or render effective an extensive democratic government such as ours, a large portion of wisdom founded upon truth and justice must necessarily circulate among the people.

Some incongruities or acts of injustice, such as are at variance with the economy of self-preservation, must ever be expected as national appendages to human imbecility and selfish passion. These may arise from neglect in cultivating the rational faculties, or from organic imperfections in those individuals: but the most glaring absurdity in ours, is the general prejudice or fashionable jealousy against complexion or difference of color, which seems singularly predominant in all our States: even so far as to neutralize or rather to hostilize the whole colored population of the Union; and that is a full fifth part of our entire population, together with at least one fifth part more of the white population, which from a natural sentiment of justice opposed to oppression is constrained to put itself in the scale of the colored people.

If so glaring an iniquity was a necessary or natural evil, essential to our physical existence, it would be wrong to mention or to make any remarks about it; but as experience is the test of truth, and proves it to be fictitious, so that we need only look round us to every other American nation or colony situated as we are, only with a much greater proportion of colored people mixed with a smaller proportion of whites, to see that this unnatural prejudice against complexion, if it does exist at all with them, is so modified and subjected to reason and justice that no perceptible evil is produced from it, but on the contrary, every advantage of natural strength and utility which any other equal portion of people could produce.

This great difference of effect is caused by a very small sacrifice of that feeling called pride or nobility of color: merely by allowing the law, criminal or civil, to operate upon all free people equally and indiscriminately.

The free colored people have never asked for more than constitutional protection to person and property; and this is granted to all free people in all civilized countries, with one exception; that exception is *the United States.*

Many humane and liberally thinking statesmen throughout the Union, feel humbled at some recent traits of severity and injustice manifested by individual State Governments, more especially when such aggravated acts of injustice originated in states where slavery was constitutionally prohibited; Ohio, for example, in its acts of oppression against its free colored inhabitants, by which their existence seems so far to have been threatened as to induce an attempt on their part to seek refuge under a foreign government, in a climate ill suited to their natural constitutions.[3]

Nothing can be further from the intention of the writer of this communication, than either to interfere with, or say any thing disrespectful concerning the acts of the great and independent State of Ohio, or of any other government in their acts of legislation; or even to enquire whether they do right or wrong. This communication merely originates in a wish to put these unfortunate objects of oppression on their guard against placing themselves rashly in a situation which, though flattering at first view, might not be permanently to their advantage.

Although the British Constitution, under which Canada is now governed, offers an ample guarantee against prejudice or injustice to *every* settler; yet Canada is only a Provincial Government, and may, at some future period not far distant, lose the advantages of that protection; which probability, when taken into consideration, and added to the extreme cold-

3. Black Laws enacted in 1804 and 1807 forced African Americans who settled in Ohio to post a $500 bond to assure their good behavior and to have a court certificate to prove that they were free. State officials did not enforce these laws until 1829, when the expanding black population in Cincinnati spurred the city authorities to invoke the Black Laws. Local blacks sent a delegation to Canada to find a location for resettlement and asked the Ohio legislature to repeal the Black Laws. White mobs drove out of Cincinnati from 1,100 to 2,200 blacks, most of whom settled in Canada. Richard C. Wade, "The Negro in Cincinnati, 1800–1830," *Journal of Negro History* 39 (January 1954): 43–57; Leon F. Litwack, *North of Slavery: The Negro in the Free States, 1790–1860* (Chicago: University of Chicago Press, 1961), 72–74.

ness of the climate, so uncongenial to the feelings of the colored people, argues strongly against the growth of a colored settlement in Canada.[4]

The consideration of the above facts would induce the writer of this, himself colored, a native of Florida, and now a resident of that Territory,[5] and feelingly alive to their success, to recommend to them to look towards Mexico as a place of safety and permanent refuge.[6] The colored people of these States are now loudly called upon by the imperious jaws of necessity and self preservation to do something in their own behalf, to mitigate, if possible, the cruel system of persecution now carrying on against them, and which, in the Southern States, threatens their very existence.

Notwithstanding that the present aspect of Mexico is unfavorable and does not at this moment offer any very great protection to industry, yet this passing political agitation with which private individuals have little to do, is perhaps only temporary, and can hardly hinder their progress as settlers which would depend upon their own industry and peaceable behavior.[7]

In the first place, it is conveniently situated, being contiguous to most of the Southern States; the climate is mild, healthy and pleasant for people of dark complexions; land, it is presumed, can be obtained from individuals upon very favorable terms, or from government *gratis*—cotton, sugar, corn or stock are soon raised where there is little or no winter to kill vegetation; the country is boundless in its extent, and either entirely uninhabited or thinly settled with people who are mostly colored *and entirely free from all prejudice against complexion.* The Constitution and laws of Mexico *recog-*

---

4. In 1829, the governor of Upper Canada declared to potential African-American settlers that the people of his province "do not know men by their color. Should you come to us you will be entitled to all the privileges of the rest of His Majesty's subjects." *Condition of the People of Color in the State of Ohio* (Boston, Mass., 1839), 7, quoted in Litwack, *North of Slavery,* 73. For black settlement in Canada, see Fred Landon, "Social Conditions among the Negroes in Upper Canada," Ontario Historical Society, *Papers and Records* 22 (1925): 144–61.

5. See n. 1 on p. 76.

6. The Republic of Mexico abolished slavery in September 1829, but in December of that year, the president exempted Texas from the prohibition against slavery.

7. After Mexico won its independence from Spain in 1821, a chaotic succession of governments ruled the new nation. Mexico was governed by an imperial followed by a federalist form of government in the 1820s. Spain tried and failed to reconquer Mexico in 1828. From 1829 to 1844, the presidency changed hands twenty times and the average duration of an administration was seven and a half months. Furthermore, controversy over the rebellious Mexican province of Texas would soon erupt into war with the United States. Gene M. Brack, *Mexico Views Manifest Destiny, 1821–1846: An Essay on the Origins of the Mexican War* (Albuquerque: University of New Mexico Press, 1975), 53–55.

nize no difference of merit on account of color,[8] between the different shades of the human race; and this gives great advantages to a dark complexion over that of a Danish or Saxon origin, which could not long endure the toil of agriculture of a warm climate.

In the second place, the vicinity of the Southern States, where the free people of color are now looking round for an asylum to relieve themselves from a situation worse than slavery, and from which they would fly to any place of refuge where the climate was congenial to their existence, and where their persons and properties were constitutionally protected or where they could peaceably exist by the fruits of their own industry.

A settlement thus located could not fail of having the support and good wishes of all the humane and liberally thinking people within the United States, or wherever the imperious causes of the migration of the colored people were known. And there are those to be found who would interest themselves in their behalf with the Mexican Government, so as to obtain lands for settlement, and who would even liberally contribute their means to promote such establishment.[9]

The first step should be, to apprize the Mexican Government of their objects and intentions, and to obtain the good wishes of the local authorities of that country, so as to protect the first emigrants in their settlement, to locate good land, where there should be a direct and convenient communi-

---

8. Contemporary testimony suggests that "skin color alone was not a major obstacle to social advancement" in Mexico. When American antislavery colonizationist Benjamin Lundy met a freed black in San Antonio in 1833, Lundy observed, "He says the Mexicans pay him the same respect as to other laboring people, there being no difference made here on account of colour." Lundy also observed that in Mexico, "amalgamation," even by marriage, was possible. Historian David J. Weber concluded that "free blacks and runaway black slaves from the United States who made their way to northern Mexico, found themselves in a society where they enjoyed juridical equality as well as tolerance of racial differences. What racial prejudice they did encounter on the Mexican frontier existed in milder form than in the United States, and seldom led to overt discrimination." David J. Weber, *The Mexican Frontier, 1821–1846: The American Southwest Under Mexico* (Albuquerque: University of New Mexico Press, 1982), 213; Benjamin Lundy, *Life, Travels and Opinions of Benjamin Lundy* (Philadelphia, Pa.: William D. Parrish, 1847; reprint, New York: Arno Press, 1969), 48; Rosalie Schwartz, *Across the Rio to Freedom: U.S. Negroes in Mexico* (El Paso: Texas Western Press, 1975), 23.

9. Perhaps Kingsley referred to Benjamin Lundy, who had supported the emigration of emancipated slaves to Haiti, helped free blacks settle in Canada, and by the early 1830s began to look to Texas as a destination for African-American emigration. Kingsley may also have been thinking here of Samuel Webb of Philadelphia, who was a friend of Joaquín María del Castillo y Lanzas, the Mexican chargé d'affaires to whom Webb wrote in 1832 asking about the settlement of free blacks in Mexico. Schwartz, *Across the Rio to Freedom*, 20; Dillon, *Benjamin Lundy*, 165–83.

cation by land or water with the United States; as well to obtain supplies and to export produce, as to facilitate the introduction of new settlers of property, who mostly live on the seaboard of the Southern States, and who would sell out their property at any sacrifice to free themselves from the state of bondage under which they now exist; for what can be greater bondage than to exist without rights, fair subjects of wanton oppression, unrecognized by any permanent protection, either legislative or constitutional?

A FREE COLORED FLORIDIAN

Memorial to Congress by Citizens of the Territory of Florida (1833)[1]

To the Honorable the Senate and house of Representatives of the United States.

The Petition of the undersigned Citizens of the Territory of Florida respectfully sheweth, that for several years past the legislation of the said Territory has been calculated materially to disturb the peace and happiness and to injure the property of the ceded inhabitants of the late provinces of Spain who are by the Treaty now Citizens of the United States. Your Petitioners are aware that the evils of which they complain have not arrisen from any thing inherent in the institutions and Laws of the United States, but have their origin in the illiberal prejudices of a local government totally at variance with the liberal spirit and generous policy of the nation and age in which we live: it will not be necessary for us in appealing to so intelligent a body as the one we address, to say that every nation and people have particular customs and habits which if not at War with the institutions of other countries are universally viewed with great toleration and indulgence. This principle has been carried so far in other countries where there was an established religion that the ceded inhabitants were permitted to retain theirs. There are doubtless some practises in all countries tolerated by National indulgencies that may not be approved by all the people of the United States; but those are diseases of the body politic to be changed by example and public sentiment and not by the nostrums of political quackery which will nauseate and disgust every one whose misfortune it has been to be transfered to the United States.

The laws to which your Memorialists chiefly object as coming under the

1. Autograph Document Signed. National Archives and Records Administration, Record Group 233, U. S. Congress, House of Representatives, 22nd Cong., 1st sess., 1833, HR22A-G23.1, Committee on Territories, Various Subjects; printed in Carter, ed., *The Territorial Papers of the United States*, 24:800–802.

designation above mentioned are mostly those of the last Session of Council relating to free people of color: it cannot have escaped the observation of your honorable body that in all slaveholding countries some portion of the population and not a very inconsiderable part have without the formalities of Marriage ceremonies, children by colored women. in all Spanish countries they were free and admitted to most of the rights of Spanish subjects especially to the natural and inherent right of legal protection from which they are now excluded: however these practices may be at variance with the national prejudices of a portion of the United States they existed in the recently aquired country and are not to be extinguished at once by intolerance and persecution or any other moral or political fanaticism: These evils are not to be rooted out by legal penalties any more than faith is to be controuled by the terrors of the Inqusition and a resort to the one is no more to be justified than to the other. The Legislative Council of Florida however acting upon the idea of bringing every thing to their own standard of moral perfection: as the Tyrant of antiquity did to His bed,[2] have denounced penalties and imposed taxes on this class of population only on account of their color: These unfortunate people are not only required to pay the usual taxes which other citizens pay but they are required to pay from five to ten dollars each on both sexes over fifteen years of age because of their color, in addition, and to be sold as slaves for life if they should be too poor to pay these odious and unequal taxes; besides being outlawed and excluded from all legal redress for injuries done either to their persons or properties: connected with this also is a law to break up all those paternal obligations and ties of natural affection which have existed for years past by imposing a fine of one thousand dollars with the penalty of disfranchisement upon every White person who is *suspected* of having a connexion with a coloured woman and the like penalty for inter-marrying with any person suspected to be of colored origin or for performing such ceremony.

The Legislative Acts of Florida are now replete with many cruel and unjust laws but those of mental persecution and proscription for the virtuous and sacred ties of domestic life and parental affection are certainly the most tyranical and the most repugnant to the free institutions of our republican government and perfect novelties in modern legislation.

---

2. In Greek mythology, Procrustes was a robber who lived on the road from Megara to Athens. He forced travelers to lie down on one of his two beds. He made the tall to lie in a short bed and sawed off their legs to make them fit, while he forced the short to lie in a long bed and stretched them violently to make them fit. Theseus later killed Procrustes using the robber's own methods. Grimal, *Dictionary of Classical Mythology*, 392.

Your Memorialists therefore humbly pray that all those cruel, unnecessary and most impolitic laws not authorised by the Constitution of the United States be repealed and annulled and your Petitioners as in duty bound will ever pray &c

Z. Kingsley

Charles W. Clarke[3]

Geo:—JF:—Clarke[4]

F: Richard[5]

Edward H Sams[6]

D. S. Gardiner[7]

F J Ross[8]

3. Charles W. Clarke (1773–c. 1840) was the brother of George J. F. Clarke. He was an adviser to Spanish officials, an officer in the militia, and a resident of St. Augustine and Fernandina. He had four sons with a free black woman, Patty Wiggins, and provided for his mulatto children. Louise Biles Hill, "George J. F. Clarke, 1774–1836," *Florida Historical Quarterly* 21 (January 1943): 207–8.

4. George J. F. Clarke (1774–1836) was the surveyor general, a militia officer, a trusted adviser to the Spanish governors of East Florida, and one of the largest landowners in Florida. He lived most of his life in St. Augustine and Fernandina. Like Kingsley, Clarke had several mulatto children: eight by a free black woman named Flora, and four by a slave named Hannah or Anna. Clarke had purchased Flora in 1793 and manumitted her in 1797. In his will, made out in St. Augustine in 1834, he made specific bequests to his brother and to Hannah/Anna and her four children. Part of the latter bequest was to be used to purchase her and their children's freedom. He instructed that the remainder of his estate be divided equally among his eight children by Flora. He had been a slaveholder earlier in his life but had conveyed the last of them to his children in 1822. Hill, "George J. F. Clarke," 197–204, 211–12.

5. Francis Richard lived in Duval County at least from 1822 to 1840. In 1840 his household included three slaves, a white woman, another white man, and a white child under five years of age. Carter, ed., *Territorial Papers of the United States,* 22:477, 24:604; Duval County, Florida, Sixth Census of the United States, 1840.

6. Edward H. Sams (b. 1780s) lived in Duval County at least from 1831 to 1840. In the latter year, he owned thirty-eight slaves. A free "colored" woman lived in his Duval County household, as did two free "colored" children under ten years of age. Carter, ed., *Territorial Papers of the United States,* 24:479; Duval County, Florida, Sixth Census of the United States, 1840.

7. Daniel S. Gardiner was a slaveholder and resided in St. Augustine in the mid-1820s. By 1831 he lived in Duval County. He was a captain in the Florida militia during the Seminole War of 1835–36. Carter, ed., *Territorial Papers of the United States,* 22:857–58; 23:159–60, 24:478; Clarence Edwin Carter, ed., *The Territorial Papers of the United States,* vol. 3, *The Territory of Florida,* 1824–28 (Washington, D.C.: Government Printing Office, 1958), 159–60.

8. Francis J. Ross (c. 1780s–1861) was a large planter who lived in Hamilton County. In 1840, his household included forty slaves and two free "colored" males. By 1845, he was the largest planter in Hamilton County, with fifty-two slaves and 1,720 acres of land. Hamilton County, Florida, Sixth Census of the United States, 1840; Julia F. Smith, "Cotton and the Factorage System in Antebellum Florida," *Florida Historical Quarterly* 49 (July 1970): 44; Dorothy Dodd, "Florida in 1845," *Florida Historical Quarterly* 24 (July 1945): 7–8.

Sam Kingsley[9]
J. A. Coffee[10]
Rocque Leonardi[11]
Ant° Lazari
Adam Cooper[12]

[*Endorsed*] Florida—Inh[ts] of Memorial To Congress complaining of certain acts of the Legislative councils—Jan[y] 28. 1833 Ref[d] to the Committee on the Territories White F. 42.[13]

9. Samuel Kingsley served as judge, justice of the peace, and postmaster for an area along the St. Johns River in Duval County. His relationship, if any, to Zephaniah Kingsley is unclear. Carter, ed., *Territorial Papers of the United States,* 23:622, 781, 982.

10. Joshua A. Coffee (b. c. 1790s) served as a surveyor for Alachua County and Indian boundary lines during the 1820s and worked out of St. Augustine. In 1831, he was a deputy surveyor for East Florida and lived in Duval County. By 1840, Coffee's Jacksonville household included two slaves and five free "colored" persons: a female aged twenty-four to thirty-six, a male and a female aged ten to twenty-four, and two males under age ten. Carter, ed., *Territorial Papers of the United States,* 23:436, 623–24, 780, 24:507, 603; Duval County, Florida, Sixth Census of the United States, 1840.

11. Rocque Leonardi (a.k.a. Roky Leonardy, b. c. 1800s) was a descendant of the Minorcan settlers who immigrated to Florida in the 1780s. Leonardi lived in St. Augustine for most, if not all, of his life. In 1840, his household included a white female aged twenty to thirty, a white female aged five to ten, a white female and two white males under age five. He also owned three slaves. St. Johns County, Florida, Sixth Census of the United States, 1840.

12. Adam Cooper lived in Nassau County at least from 1831 to 1840. In 1840, he and another white male lived with six free "colored" people, three of whom were children. Cooper had no slaves in 1840. Carter, ed., *Territorial Papers of the United States,* 24:600; Nassau County, Florida, Sixth Census of the United States, 1840.

13. "Mr. White, of Florida, presented a memorial of inhabitants of the Territory of Florida, praying that certain acts of the Legislative Council of that Territory relating to free people of color, may be annulled by Congress, which memorial was referred to the Committee on Territories." 28 January 1833, U. S. Congress, House, *Journal,* 22d Cong., 2d sess., 1832, 246. Joseph M. White was the territorial delegate from Florida to Congress.

Letters On Haiti (1835, 1838)[1]

The Letters which follow are from the Working Man's Advocate,[2] the editor of which paper introduces the first of them by saying—"The following Letter from an intelligent and philanthropic southern gentleman (though a large slaveholder) now travelling in Haiti, will doubtless convey much information to our readers respecting the present political condition and natural advantages of that interesting Island. The statements of the writer may be implicitly relied on."

1. Printed Letter(s). *The Rural Code of Haiti, Literally Translated from a Publication by the Government Press; Together with Letters from that Country, Concerning Its Present Condition, By a Southern Planter* (Granville, Middletown, N.J.: George H. Evans, 1837), 35–48; 3d ed. (New York: J. Vale, 1839).
    The first two-thirds of this forty-eight-page pamphlet consists of six laws proposed by President Jean Pierre Boyer of Haiti and passed by the Chamber of the Representatives of Communes in 1826. Together, these six laws (containing 202 articles) made up the "Rural Code of Haiti." Because agriculture was "the main source of the prosperity of the state," Boyer designed these laws to reinvigorate Haiti's agricultural economy by making plantation work for laborers obligatory. However, the strict policies to prohibit vagrancy and to enforce agricultural labor were never fully implemented. *The Rural Code of Haiti*, 3; Frank Moya Pons, "Haiti and Santo Domingo, 1790–c. 1870," in Bethell, ed., *The Cambridge History of Latin America*, 3:260–61.
    The first edition of the pamphlet includes four letters written by Kingsley from Haiti in 1835. The third edition also includes his 1838 letter. The publisher, George H. Evans, was also the editor of the *Working Man's Advocate*, in which the first four letters appeared beginning in October 1835. In an "advertisement" within the pamphlet itself, Evans wrote, "This pamphlet was put to press more than a year ago, but its publication was delayed by unforseen causes. It is thought, however, that the present time is no less propitious for the promulgation of the information it contains than the former period, since it is every day becoming more apparent, that the increase of the colored population of the United States forbodes an evil, which a large portion of the people are evidently anxious to avoid."
    2. See n. 2 on p. 76.

LETTER I.[3]

Puerto de Plata, Haiti,[4] 13th Sept., 1835.

Mr. George H. Evans:[5]

Dear Sir—When I left New York, about a month ago, with the intention of spending the hot season of summer under the cool shade of the plantain and royal palm trees, fanned by the sea breezes of the healthy and temperate climate of Hayti, I promised to convey to you, as soon and as intelligibly as I could, a true description of what I saw in my progress through this Island of Liberty, which, although hardly two week's sail from New York, must become of great political importance, but is now quite unknown, even by name, to nine-tenths of our New York citizens.

On the 3d inst., being nearly 20° N. lat., we made the Island of Haiti. It resembled the Catskill mountains, only more extended. On the 4th we sailed into a harbor on its N. side, called Puerto de Plata, where we found American and foreign shipping anchored before a pretty, scattered-looking small town of one story houses, something about the size of St. Augustine. We landed soon after, amidst logs of mahogany, in which, and tobacco in bales, most of its export consists. The poor appearance of the town was

3. This letter first appeared in the *Working Man's Advocate* on October 17, 1835, under the title "Facts Respecting Haiti." The version published in pamphlet form and presented here differed only in capitalization and punctuation from the newspaper version, except where noted.

4. Puerto de Plata, on the northern coast of the island, was in the Spanish portion that had been Santo Domingo before 1822 and would become the Dominican Republic in 1844. For free black migration to Puerto Plata in the nineteenth century, see José Augusto Puig Ortiz, *Emigracion de Libertos Norteamericanos a Puerto Plata en la Primera Mitad del Siglo XIX* (Dominican Republic: Editora Alfa y Omega, 1978).

5. George Henry Evans was born in England. In New York, he actively supported the radical Working Men's Movement and Robert Dale Owen's efforts on behalf of educational reform. A social radical and a deist, he came to support the Jacksonian Democrats when the initial labor radicalism dwindled. Evans condemned the July 1834 antiabolitionist riot in New York and later declared that he supported the abolition of slavery. By 1835, he was part of a division in Democratic ranks and the creation of an Equal Rights (or Loco Foco) party. In addition to editing and publishing the *Working Man's Advocate,* he also printed Owen's *Free Enquirer* for a time and published the first edition of Kingsley's *The Rural Code of Haiti, Literally Translated from a Publication by the Government Press; Together with Letters from that Country, Concerning Its Present Condition, By a Southern Planter* in 1837. After suspending publication of the *Working Man's Advocate* in 1836, Evans began publication of a monthly journal titled *The Radical* in 1841, which advocated land reform. Wilentz, *Chants Democratic,* 182, 209, 212, 336.

amply compensated for by the rich verdure of the waving cocoa nut and majestic palm trees, growing on the gently rising plain which lays between the town and the mountain, (called Torre de Isabella,) majestically rising behind it, to the height of three thousand feet, and richly covered with trees to the top.

This afternoon and next day, I was occupied in walking about the town, and gardens in its vicinity, and in cultivating the acquaintance of its inhabitants, who received me, as a white stranger, with great civility as well as hospitality. They consisted of white and black, (the latter predominated,) speaking Spanish, French, and English, as languages common to all, the Spanish rather the most, and the white part of the population very much resembled the Minoroian population of St. Augustine.[6] The beautiful and rich plain on which the town is built, of two miles in extent, and gradually rising to the foot of the mountain of La Torre, contains first the town and gardens, and then some small farms, cultivated with sugar cane, coffee, oranges, mangoes, corn, yams, potatoes, cassava, and all kinds of fancy produce, to suit the market, and for the supply of the town. The low lands between the sea and the mountains, extend to the east and to the west as far as the eye can reach; and if the soil is a fair sample of the soil of this Island, which, from all that I can hear, is probable, there is nothing that I have ever seen in any country, not even the low lands of the Mississippi, nor the alluvial deposits of Guiana, in South America, equal it in fertility. The sugar cane grows to a prodigious size, and lasts for twenty years without replanting. The plantain, as food for man, is the richest of nature's gifts, and also perpetuates itself, with little attention, for an equal period of time without replanting. Groves of cocoa nut and royal palm trees, the most magnificent of nature's productions, shade the ground with their waving tops, and furnish food for countless numbers of wild hogs, cattle, &c.; wild guinea fowls also are very abundant. 6th September, being Sunday, I this morning went to hear mass in a very large church of one story, which safe mode of building,

6. In 1768, Dr. Andrew Turnbull settled approximately 1,400 Minorcans, Corsicans, Italians, and Greeks at New Smyrna, several miles south of St. Augustine on the Florida coast. Working as indentured servants for ten years on Turnbull's indigo plantations, these settlers suffered deprivations and harsh discipline. Within two years, half of the settlers died. In 1777, the remaining settlers migrated to St. Augustine, where they supplemented the ethnic diversity of the town. Most of the settlers of New Smyrna remained in East Florida when the British evacuated in 1784. The Minorcan, Greek, and Italian settlers of New Smyrna became loyal Spanish settlers. E. P. Panagopoulos, *New Smyrna: An Eighteenth Century Greek Odyssey* (Gainesville: University of Florida Press, 1966).

I presume, is on account of earthquakes that sometimes[7] happen here. The audience was large and most respectable, the female part especially was devout, and would bear comparison, in point of good looks or dress, with any of our white congregations in New York. In the evening I went to hear an old style methodist sermon, by an English missionary, where most of our poor American colored emigrants were assembled, to hear themselves denounced as fit subjects for a very necessary personage, now dormant in fashionable life, but all went off well: we had no *mob*.

13th. I have now been here ten days, and have closely examined the country on horseback, twelve leagues of coast and three leagues inland, to the summit ridges, where they cut[8] mahogany; no sentry has ever hailed me, no officer of police has ever enquired into my business, or what I wanted. I brought no letter of introduction: which ever way I travelled, I have been treated with hospitality and attention, and all possible kindness rendered to me voluntarily and without reward. I have had a hearty welcome every where, abundance to eat, and a place to hang my hammock at night, from black and poor colored people, who live insolated [isolated], upon small farms of one family, scattered within the rich, uncut forests of Haiti, where their living in simple abundance and with little labor does not detract from their natural kindness of heart, which sustains their practical moral merit of character; for notwithstanding our fashionable propensity for aviliating[9] the merit of color, no one has ever cited one solitary instance of a breach of honesty, or honorable hospitality to any white man or other person. A single unarmed foot man is the only conveyance of money remittances from here to Port-au-Prince, a distance of nearly one hundred leagues, mostly through solitary woods; but no instance is recorded of either robbery, murder, or insult. Further comment upon natural kindness of heart is needless. I have not heard of any other instance similar in any country, or under any government—here every appearance indicates perfect freedom and equality without law or restraint; yet no one trespasses upon the strictest laws of decorum and politeness.

Many of our pseudo republicans openly abuse Haiti, its people and government, but here they read our newspapers, and daily accounts of mobs,

7. The original newspaper version of the letter used the word "seldom" instead of "sometimes" here.

8. The original newspaper version of the letter included "and hawl" here.

9. *Aviliating* seems to be Kingsley's derivative of the verb *avile*, which means *to depreciate* or *to vilify*. *Oxford English Dictionary*, 2d ed. (Oxford: Clarendon Press, 1989), 1:821.

and persecution of color, without any symptom of resentment or anger against the citizens of those very countries where their color is outlawed, and who enjoy every protection, both of person and property, in Haiti. Although many families here are white in all their relations, I have never seen nor heard of any slight or symptom of *natural* prejudice against color; indeed, as a white man, I feel ashamed to receive such kindness and hospitality from the very people, whom public prejudice, or rather fashion or jealousy, in New York, would exclude from obtaining necessary refreshment at an inn, or from travelling in any public conveyance or vehicle, or even to walk the streets but as outlawed miscreants. The state of society here proves very clearly to me, that our main argument to excuse our persecution of color, (natural prejudice of caste,) if unsupported by law, soon melts, and is dissolved by our moral relations, if let alone, like any other legal privilege. Privileged grades of society are necessary to the existence of a regal aristocracy, or of a popular democracy or oligarchy: annul the privileges and these governments become republican, or of equal laws. This government of Haiti approaches nearer to pure republicanism than any other, now in use or on record. Although the aggregate population of this island may approach towards a million of people, yet it is hardly possible to find a servant to hire, which is easy to account for from the circumstance that every colored person of good character is a citizen from the moment of his arrival, and upon application to the Commandant, can have as much good land, gratis, from the government, as he thinks he can cultivate; therefore no one will hire, and the quantity of population and small farms of one family each, is fast increasing. To gain information where every thing is new, I have reposed but little in the shade since my arrival, but the air is delightfully cool every night and morning, and during the day, while travelling, I have suffered but little from the heat, as our roads lay through lofty thick woods, the shade of which completely excluded the solar rays. We generally have had a refreshing shower every day, and I feel my health much improved since my arrival from New York, nor can I hear of a single instance of sickness any where, although this is called the sickly season, and if I can judge from the number of children playing about in the streets and houses, the population must be increasing very rapidly. In a few days I propose continuing my journey west, towards Cape Haïtien, formerly Cape Français, and will, from thence, communicate what may seem new.

I remain, &c.

LETTER II.[10]

Cape Haïtien,[11] 29th Sept., 1835.

MR. GEORGE H. EVANS:

DEAR SIR—In my last letter, from Puerto de Plata, I endeavored to give you a short description of that place and its vicinity. Since that time I have rode on horseback, in company with one person and a guide, to this place, where I now am in good health, a distance of two hundred miles or more, chiefly within a few miles of the coast, through an uninterrupted scenery of the most romantic order, sometimes over level and very extensive prairie pasturages, well peopled with the finest cattle I ever saw, mixed here and there with flocks of sheep and goats, and every where abounding with wild guinea fowls; at other times we crossed clear and rapid streams of water, coming from between the mountains, situated a few miles further in the interior, and of an height seldom less than one, or more than three thousand feet, and thickly wooded to the top. This space between the sea and the mountains, of about two or three leagues wide, is a rich alluvial valley, gradually rising from the sea to the foot of the mountains, which are also very fertile and well wooded, and lay convenient for cultivation. This valley of level land is interrupted in two places by mountainous ridges, which extend down to the sea, one immediately below Puerto de Plata, the other at Point Isabellique. In most places the luxuriant growth of timber was thickly interspersed with the elegant royal palm, and covered a deep soil of incomparable richness and fertility, mostly convenient to water power for machinery. That part of the island formerly Spanish, terminates at a flourishing and romantic little town called Laxavon, which is watered by the river Massacre. This river formed the boundary line between the former Spanish and French possessions of St. Domingo; it falls into the sea a small distance east of Fort Dauphin, now Fort Libertié, which lays fifteen miles to the S.W., and is a very extensive well laid out town, conveniently watered by a clear river, which flows partly around it. The houses are elegantly built of stone, and covered with French tiles; many of them, however, have been

---

10. This letter first appeared in the *Working Man's Advocate* on October 31, 1835, under the title "Letters on Haiti—No. II." The version published in pamphlet form and presented here differed only in capitalization and punctuation from the newspaper version, except where noted.

11. Cape Haïtien, on the northern coast, was in the Department of the North in the Republic of Haiti, in the French-speaking western third of the island.

taken down and removed, to furnish materials for other buildings. Its harbor is excellent, and superior, I believe, to any other on the whole island. Here begins the famous Plain of the Cape, 36 miles distant, through which its wide, level, and well laid out road, bordered with high, shady logwood hedges, still exists; in some parts it passed over pasturage or prairie lands, but generally, the massy remains of extensive stone buildings indicated the value of the soil of its former sugar plantations, now mostly grown up with woods. Many old plantations are still more or less under the cultivation of sugar, but the extreme scarcity of hands to hire, renders the extensive cultivation of that staple at present impracticable.

Passing through the very rich and extensive alluvial plantations of the Grand Riviere, we arrived at Cape Haïtien, about nine miles distant from it. This City (formerly Cape Français,) is built on a level plain, just under a romantic mountain, of perhaps 2000 feet high. The great extent and magnificent remains of elegant and extensive stone buildings indicate its former wealth, founded upon the richness and extent of its soil, when it stood the peerless Mistress of American opulence. It seems now recovering a little its importance, which will no doubt keep pace with the present increase of population and cultivation throughout the island.

Excepting Saturdays and Sundays, the great market days, when all is alive with well dressed good-looking people, few persons are to be seen in the streets. This is owing to the great scarcity of domestic servants, who can employ themselves more profitably upon their own lands, liberally bestowed by government, whose policy it is to discourage all negative and unproductive occupations.

I will now close this letter by a few observations upon the people inhabiting the country between Puerto de Plata and Cape Haïtien, their complexion, moral habits, etc. In that part formerly Spanish, that language is still retained, though the French is generally understood, and must soon predominate, as the law requires that all records and public documents shall be kept in French. A great tendency to white is also observable in the complexions of the people, which seem to be changing very fast by intermixture with color. Soon after crossing the river Massacre, the French language predominates, or rather the Creole, for both are spoken and generally understood. The complexions of the inhabitants, too, are generally darker, indicating a greater predominancy of African blood, but no general color can be said to characterize any section. The extremes of white and black, when divested of all legal preference as in Haïti, are more commonly found in conjugal union than otherwise, and as no distinctive predilection of color has yet manifested itself, the national complexion is continually changing, and must finally depend upon the sources of population from whence the color is derived.

I found no tavern or public house on the whole road—we lodged wherever circumstances rendered it most convenient to stop. Every where we found gratuitous hospitality and welcome, with an abundant supply of wholesome provisions, such as pork, fowls, honey, corn, cassava bread, and delicious plantains and fruit. The lonesome and romantic woods were interspersed with small farms of one family each, all living in careless abundance, and full of healthy children. Some of the towns had a more fashionable and military appearance, and it seemed to be a general custom of every Commandant to assume the prerogative right of offering hospitality to strangers, and where we met, not only a friendly welcome, but genteel and fashionable accommodations. No tale of robbery or personal insult could be heard of. The houses of these farms are of the most simple construction, with posts of durable wood set in the ground, and wattled or enclosed with palm-tree clapboards, and generally covered with the same; they were mostly open, so as to allow a free circulation of the cool breezes of this healthy climate. I neither have seen nor heard of one instance of sickness as yet, nor any kind of indisposition, in my whole route. They appear to be a healthy and good looking people, and in the towns fashionable, with many women of excellent beauty. I could discover no prejudice of caste, although whites seemed rather to be treated with most deference, which I imputed either to their being considered as more helpless, or their being supposed to have the most money; but all seemed to mix together equally in society, which was regulated by the conditions of the individuals only.

My next communication will probably be dated from Port-au-Prince, and will contain such new matter as may grow out of further observation.

I remain, very respectfully, &c.

LETTER III.[12]

Port-au-Prince,[13] Oct. 12th, 1835.

12. This letter first appeared in the *Working Man's Advocate* on November 21, 1835, under the title "Letters from Haiti—No. III." The version published in pamphlet form and presented here differed only in capitalization and punctuation from the newspaper version, except where noted.

13. Port-au-Prince, located in the Department of the South on the western coast of the island, was the capital of the Republic of Haiti.

MR. GEORGE H. EVANS—

My last letter was from Cape Haïtien, which we left on horseback for Gonaïves, a distance of about 65 miles to the westward, with one colored attendant. The first part of our way was up the beautiful vale of the Cape and river Saleé, through ruins of extensive mason work, and old plantations, now but little cultivated. The road lead towards the conspicuous and elevated palace and village of Sans Soucie, situated near the top of a well cultivated mountain on our left. After leaving this plain, and ascending a moderate elevation, we came in sight of the fine plain and harbor of Limbé, into which a beautiful river of the same name falls, up the valley of the south branch of which, with many crossings, we ascended to the small and romantic valley of Camp Cog, surrounded by richly wooded hills; here we were hospitably entertained for the night: early next morning we continued our route up this romantic valley, thickly settled with small coffee farms of one family each to its top, from which we had a very interesting view of the happy vale which we had just ascended; then crossing this height of land and descending a few miles westerly, to the other or main branch of the Limbé river, upon which is situated the lively village of Plaisance, whose healthy and elevated situation, with its fertile fields and well stored gardens of fruit and vegetables, afforded an interesting picture of substantial plenty amid tropical ease and fecundity. Leaving this valley of the river, we ascended another elevation, to the height of land at the escalence or ladder, down which we descended through a grand chasm composed of perpendicular layers of limestone work fringed with calcarious [calcareous] crystals, many hundred feet in height, at the foot of which we had a view of the river and very extensive plain of the Gonaïves, which lay before us. The town is about six leagues distant from this place, on our way to which, we again saw many massy remains of cotton and sugar plantations, whose costly mason work indicated the intrinsic value of the soil for the cultivation of which they had been erected.

We arrived at the town of Gonaïves about 4 o'clock P.M. It is still important, and derives some benefit from its salt pond. The fine mahogany, floated down the great river of Artibonite, laying a few miles to the southward, loads a great many vessels, and contributes also to its prosperity.

The small coaster in which we were crowded, for two days and three nights, on our passage from Gonaïves to Port-au-Prince, along with a good many Haïtien passengers of different shades and sexes, but all upon an equal footing, afforded a good opportunity for displaying the manners and estimating the degree of civilization attained by this new people, of whom the female part seemed perfectly at their ease, and full of laughter and good humor. The male part was more musical, and often, in the intervals between stories of wars and battles, in which they had had an opportunity of showing their prowess, (for all the Haïtiens are soldiers) exercised their fine voices in singing favorite airs of good taste, and some national songs with great melody and effect. I heard nothing like vulgarity or abusive language amongst them.

On the 11th Oct., we landed at Port-au-Prince, which being the seat of Government is considered the capital of Haïti, and being Sunday, their great market and parade day made it a novel sight for a stranger from the American States. The superabundant variety of provisions of every description for the supply of the ensuing week, brought in profusion by great numbers of small craft, and innumerable horse and jackass loads of all kinds of tropical fruit and country produce, chiefly conducted by women, mixed with some good looking men, all of whom were colored, whose dark and robust arms, contrasted with the clean and snow white clothes of the females, all full of gaiety and good health, gave no unfavorable idea of the happy circumstances and substantial prosperity[14] of this agricultural community. I will take this opportunity to say, that I have never before, in any country, seen such general indications of personal cleanliness and taste in dress, as I have observed among these Haïtien women, amongst whom, the eastern customs of ablution, handed down from their African ancestors, are religiously observed; nor do I think that there is any civilized country now known to us, where substantial freedom and happiness, unalloyed by licentiousness, or any dread of injury to person or property, are enjoyed to the same extent as in Haïti; for, whether you reside in the towns, or travel alone through the country or over the mountains, by night or by day, whether you are armed or unarmed, white or black, on foot or on horseback, loaded with doubloons or with sour oranges, you are equally safe from injury. I can hear of no instance of exception. I must now have travelled by land more than 300 miles through the interior, and mostly in company with a genteel dressed man of color; and I naturally expected that a white person, and especially a stranger from the United States, would experience from the lower order of people at least, who were all colored or black, and living under a colored government, some small slight or sign of neglect, or have his feelings in some way insulted by their resentment, for I naturally felt conscious of the persecution and open war now carrying on against them in the United States,

14. The original newspaper version of the letter used the word "happiness" instead of "prosperity" here.

which I had just left; but I must confess that I felt humbled and ashamed at the undeserved respect and deference with which I, as a white man, was every where treated and received.

Oct. 17.—This day I had a long and familiar interview with President Boyer, who is a very intelligent and sensible man, and I think of great integrity and patriotism.[15] He is of the middle size and rather dark complexion, his manners are easy and polite, many of his generals and military officers were near his person, and, being Sunday, seven regiments of regular troops, besides some cavalry, with fine music, were reviewed on a very extensive and even parade ground behind the Government House; this is a part of 33 regiments of regular infantry and one regiment of cavalry, besides 4 regiments of artillery, &c., all paid by government, now composing the standing army of this island: but while we admire the officers, men, their clothing, arms, and discipline, &c., all excellent in a military point of view, we cannot help regretting the cause of this display of military pomp and expense in a time of peace, caused, it is said, by the fear of enemies from without; but as this danger seems gradually subsiding, while the agricultural capital and population of the island are rapidly increasing, in a short time it is probable that the standing army, now said to be diminishing, will be reduced to the actual wants and internal circumstances of the government. The navy is small, and consists of a few vessels of war and revenue cutters, merely to assist in the transportation of government stores, and the protection of the revenue. The militia troops are well armed and all mustered in uniform once every three months; they consist of one hundred thousand effective men, but as their muster takes place on Sunday, and in the parishes where they reside, no time is lost by their military parade.

The city of Port-au-Prince has an excellent harbor; it is mostly built of wood, and situated on a regular declivity, having high land aback, whose springs and rivulets supply its numerous fountains with abundance of excel-

---

15. Jean Pierre Boyer (1776–1850) was a free mulatto who fought with Toussaint Louverture in the revolution against French rule. He later joined André Rigaud in an abortive attempt to overthrow Louverture. In 1802 Boyer returned with Leclerc's French army but soon joined the Haitian patriots. After the assassination of Jean-Jacques Dessalines in 1806, Alexandre Pétion (1770–1818) ruled the South of a divided Haiti and Emperor Henri Christophe (1767–1820) ruled the North. Pétion chose Boyer as his successor as president for life, and Boyer reunited northern and southern Haiti after Christophe committed suicide in 1820. Local inhabitants of Spanish Santo Domingo had revolted against Haitian rule in 1808–9 and restored Spanish rule. In 1822, Boyer took advantage of weakening Spanish control of Santo Domingo and united the entire island under his government. He abolished slavery in the eastern two-thirds of the island and offered land to all the freedmen. Boyer's labor policies led Haitians to overthrow and exile him in 1843.

lent water; the lowermost fountain, which is built out in the harbor, where the water is of sufficient depth, supplies the vessels with water without unloading the casks. Its streets are broad and regularly laid out with side walks, mostly under cover of piazas, where many well dressed females sit and enjoy the cool breeze before their numerous shops of various wares, for the supply of customers. There are three large market squares, embellished with fountains, &c., and the streets near the harbor, where the custom house is, indicates a good deal of commercial hustle, by the discharging of numerous coasters, and loading and unloading of 15 or 20 foreign square rigged vessels, which usually are seen in port at the same time. I have heard of no late census of the population of Haïti, but the general estimate of the inhabitants is about one million, and it certainly is increasing most rapidly. The extraordinary fertility of its soil, fitted for all sorts of produce; the convenient temperature of its climate, which, at the sea side in summer, generally ranges from 80° to 90°, and in the interior between 75° and 85° Farenheit; (in winter it is ten degrees lower;) its extreme salubrity, its convenient situation for commerce, both as relates to Europe and to North and South America, together with all the West India Islands; its numerous and spacious ports and harbors, cannot fail, under its present free and well organized government, of bringing it, in a few years, to a state of enviable prosperity; to say that riches would increase its happiness, would be contrary to human experience, for I doubt whether in the known world another example of a country of such extent can be found, where there is so little crime, and so little human suffering as now exists within the Island of Haïti, which exults in freedom and plenty; and it would be flattering to humanity to see it prosper, after sacrificing so many lives, and fighting its way through such extraordinary obstacles, to liberty and independence, which it now temperately enjoys, without abuse or licentiousness.

Oct. 26.—As I have now been travelling in this island for two months, and studying the theory of its situation, I will, by way of closing my remarks, give you the following abbreviated view of my information.

The Island of Haïti is about 100 leagues in length, from east to west, its north side lays in 20° north latitude, the sea coast generally is low, the soil extremely rich, but rising gradually for several leagues inland, becomes more steep, and terminates in mountains richly wooded to the top. These, by arresting the clouds and rain, give rise to numerous rivers, which, after irrigating these rich plains below, fall into the surrounding ocean. Those ridges of mountains are of great extent, from east to west: the central ranges being from 5 to 7000 feet high, are intersected, lengthways, by wide valleys of rich land and extensive pasturages between them, watered by large and rapid rivers, convenient for floating down mahogany and other produce, four of which, especially, after running longitudinally for several hundred miles each, between those different ranges of mountains, and intersecting the streams of the whole interior, fall into the sea at four opposite parts of the island.

Owing to the great extent of this island, and the want of capital, the price of lands is extremely low, and many superb and costly old plantations, with all their improvements and imperishable buildings of brick and stone, together with their valuable mill streams and water privileges convenient to towns, are to be purchased for a small part of what the improvements alone would cost. No country, perhaps, in the world is so little annoyed with noxious animals or insects; very few flies or mosquetoes; very few birds of prey; no wild carnivorous animal bigger than a rat, nor any venomous snake or reptile, is to be found upon it.

In short it is a most salubrious place of residence, and offers every variety of climate, and I can see no opposing circumstance to the immediate development of the natural power and wealth of Haïti but its want of capital, the introduction of which, must depend upon the policy of its government, which, from every appearance, is now fast approaching towards the accomplishment of that object.

LETTER IV.

New York, 13th Nov., 1835.

MR. GEORGE H. EVANS:

DEAR SIR—I here enclose sundry interrogatories put to the President of Haïti, with his answers thereto. I wrote three letters to you from Haïti, one from Puerto de Plata, one from Cape Haïtien, and one from Port-au-Prince, and now, these interrogatories.

I remain, &c.

Translation of a letter from the Secretary General of the Republic of Haïti, to a Citizen of the United States, in answer to a letter to his Excellency Jean P. Boyer, President of that Republic, requiring information upon the subject of emigrants from the United States.

SIR—His Excellency, the President of Haïti, orders me to answer the questions contained in two letters, which you addressed to him on the 15th of this month of October, 1835, regarding the introduction into this republic of some people of African descent, who propose emigrating from the United States of America, where they now inhabit.[16]

On purpose that the answers may reply fully to the questions, I shall, Sir, arrange the translations of these questions in the same order as you have placed them.

1st Ques. For how long a period of time, and upon what conditions, could such emigrants contract with their servants abroad, as mechanics or agricultural laborers in Haïti, so that such contracts may be held legal, and guaranteed by the Haïtien Government, after the arrival of the parties in Haïti, and how many working days in each week, and how many working hours each day, would be held legal in said contract?

Ans. To answer your first question, Sir, I refer you to the Law No. 3, page 11, of the Rural Code of Haïti, of which I now send you a copy, and to legalize any contract passed in a foreign country, between the emigrant and his servants, it will be sufficient that they appear, upon their arrival in Haïti, before a Justice of Peace, and that they mutually declare that the clauses set forth in the contract have been consented to of their own free will; and that the parties are mutually willing to execute them according to their form and tenor. All legal acts can be executed by virtue of the laws of the Republic.[17]

2d Ques. At what age could hired servants enter into such contracts in their own behalf, and for how many years afterwards, and what would be considered as a reasonable compensation or gratuity over and above such services?

Ans. To the second question I answer that the fixed age of majority is 21 years, or that of emancipation, which are clearly established in our civil code—they give the right to our citizens, or to those who are constitutionally enabled to become such, to contract in their own proper name and behalf, and the article 46 of the Rural Code fixes the duration of the time for which they can contract, whether as agriculturalists or mechanics."[18]

---

*Kingsley's Note: "The extent is 9 years—at 15 years they can contract through the act of their parents or guardians for 9 years, and in the same way children may be bound until 21 years. A note or bond may be taken from the party as a further security for the fulfilment of such contracts."

---

16. On African-American migration from the U.S. to Haiti in the 1820s and 1830s, see Dillon, *Benjamin Lundy,* 87–103, and Hunt, *Haiti's Influence on Antebellum America,* 165–73.

17. The reference is to Articles 45 through 47 of Law Number III of the Rural Code. Those "whose profession it is to cultivate the ground" were obliged to enter into contracts with landowners "either collectively or individually." The contracts could have a duration of from two to nine years. *The Rural Code of Haiti,* 10.

18. Article 46 specified that contracts were to be from two to nine years for those employed

3d Ques. By what authority could children under age be bound, and until what age would such agricultural apprenticeship be binding in Haïti, upon those apprentices, so as to indemnify the emigrants for the passages, losses, &c.

Ans. To the 3d question I answer, that the fathers and mothers, and, in their absence, the parents in direct line, and in their absence, the guardians or tutors, can contract for such minors, and bind them until the age of majority or 21 years.

4th Ques. Would the government of Haïti be disposed to grant lands to such emigrants near a landing on the coast, where, and how much?

Ans. I answer to the fourth question, that since the 1st of May, 1826, the law has put an end to gratuitous commissions of lands, which composed a part of the public domain;[19] but that the government of Haïti now rents or causes to be sold, such lands as belong to the State, so that such emigrants as have a right to become Haïtiens, according to article 44 of the Constitution, may either rent or purchase such lands as they wish, whether it be from the Republic, or from the individuals who possess them.

5th Ques. Would any duties of importation be charged by government upon such property belonging to emigrants, as was not for sale, but merely intended for the agricultural or domestic purposes of such emigrants.

Ans. To answer the 5th question, I will say to you, that no duty of importation or entry will be imposed upon the moveable property of emigrants intended for their own use, or for their agricultural pursuits, or for the exercise of their mechanical professions.

6th Ques. Would colored* emigrants be allowed to purchase land and locate themselves any where within the Island of Haïti?

Ans. The question put by the 6th article will be answered by that given to 4th article. The descendants of African emigrants may locate themselves within the Republic, any where they may judge most suitable to their inter-

*Kingsley's Note: "The word colored means every person not white."

---

in "the secondary branch of cultivation and manufactures," from three to nine years for those in other branches of cultivation, and from six months to a year "for the cutting of wood for exportation." The "principal branch of cultivation" was "the raising of plants and trees yielding produce for exportation to foreign countries, grain of all descriptions, and all kinds of food and roots designed for the subsistence of the population." The secondary branch of cultivation was "the culture merely of pot herbs, of flowers, of fruit trees, of provisions, and of fodder" on plantations not established for the principal branch of cultivation. *The Rural Code of Haiti,* 8, 10.

19. See n. 42 on p. 74.

ests, and may hold real property when, after one year's residence in Haïti, they become citizens of the Republic.

7th Ques. How long a time would emigrants be allowed to go or come as foreigners before they were liable to the duties and constraints of citizens.

Ans. I answer the 7th question, that entrance into the Republic being free, to every one who will submit to the laws, the Africans or their descendants who intend to emigrate may go and come freely, in doing their business, as foreigners, but from the time they may determine to remain within the Republic, they ought to conform themselves to the 14th article of the civil code, for the security of their future rights.

8th Ques. Would government be disposed to grant a licence to a foreign vessel to enter or anchor in any bay or harbor on the north side of this island, under the direction of a colored emigrant, for the purpose of examining lands, and choosing a place for settlement?

Ans. In answer to the 8th question, I am ordered to tell you, that instructions will be sent to the military authorities all round the shores on the north east side of the Republic to permit emigrants for Haïti to land, to visit the country and to examine such lands as may appear suitable for their purposes, and to settle upon them, according to the arrangements which they may make with their several proprietors.

9th Ques. Would apprentices, introduced into Haïti as before mentioned, be liable to the same military duties as other free emigrants, who had contracted no obligation of labor before their introduction?—What would be the duties of both? or either?—Could either of them be forced into the regular army without their own consent?

Ans. Finally, sir, to answer your 9th question, I am ordered to tell you, that neither the emigrants nor any person of African descent, whom they may bring along with them to work, whether as mechanics or cultivators, will be in any manner required or held liable to do military duty as regular soldiers of the Republic. With regard to the proprietors, after one year's residence, they will be considered as forming a part of the Militia in the district where they reside. I ought to observe to you that the National Guard, or Militia, is liable to no other service but such as is mentioned in the law, of which I now send you a copy, and which consists in a simple muster every three months, on purpose to inspect the state of the arms, with which every citizen ought to be provided, for the security of his liberties, and to maintain the independence of his country.

Signed   B. INGENAC

HAÏTI.[20]

We copy the following from the Christian Statesman: The editor says, it is from a very intelligent source, and will be interesting to all who desire the prosperity of that island.

WASHINGTON, June 30, 1838.[21]

To the Editor of the Christian Statesman:[22]

SIR,—Your being one of the principal members of the African Colonization Society, an institution purely philanthropic, and whose object apparently is to advance the depressed free people of color to a higher grade in the scale of civilization; and as I am a planter in the south, deriving my entire subsistence from slave labor, but having a colored family and children, motives of necessity and self-preservation have induced me to labor for a similar object to yours in which I have been employed for some time past; therefore, as wisdom is most certainly attained from comparing the facts proved by experiment, I thought that it would be interesting to you and to many of your readers, to be informed of the result of my Colonization experiments, made in the Island of Haiti, the convenient situation of which and its nearness to the place where the emigrants lived, induced me to give it a preference.[23] A full account of these experiments follows, and their importance may excuse the length of this communication.

20. This letter first appeared in the *Christian Statesman* (Washington, D.C.) on July 6, 1838. The version published in pamphlet form and presented here differed only in capitalization and punctuation from the newspaper version, except where noted.

21. In the original newspaper version of the letter, the location from which Kingsley wrote was "Hayti" rather than Washington, and the date was June 30, 1837, an obvious typesetting error. The correct date is 1838.

22. The Reverend R. R. [Ralph Randolph] Gurley was the editor of the *Christian Statesman.* A native of Connecticut and a graduate of Yale, Gurley joined the staff of the central office of the American Colonization Society in 1822, and became the secretary of the society in June 1825. From 1822 to 1840, Gurley kept the advocates of colonization from throughout the United States together. Fox, *The American Colonization Society,* 73–74; Tise, *Proslavery,* 52–53.

23. That Kingsley identifies himself with the aims of the American Colonization Society both demonstrates how he differed from other proslavery theorists and emphasizes the ideological distance he had traveled in his own views by 1838. Most proslavery advocates insisted that African Americans were inherently inferior mentally to whites and were alarmed by the American Colonization Society's confidence in black abilities. Egerton, "Averting a Crisis," 142–56.

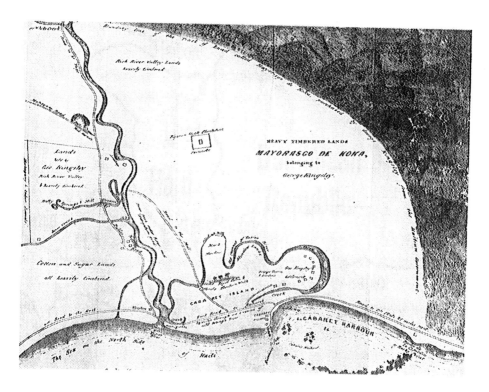

Figure 4. Map of George Kingsley's settlement, Mayorasgo de Koka, on the northern coast of Haiti, now part of the Dominican Republic. By permission of the P. K. Yonge Library of Florida History, University of Florida, Gainesville.

About eighteen months ago, I carried out my son, George Kingsley, a healthy colored man of uncorrupted morals, about thirty years of age, tolerably well educated, of very industrious habits, and a native of Florida, together with six prime African men, my own slaves, liberated for that express purpose, to the northeast side of the island of Haïti, near Port Plate, where we arrived in the month of October, 1836, and after application to the local authorities, from whom I rented some good land near the sea, and thickly timbered with lofty woods, I set them to work cutting down trees about the middle of November, and returned home to Florida. My son wrote to us frequently, giving an account of his progress. Some of the fallen timber was dry enough to burn off in January, 1837, when it was cleared up, and eight acres of corn planted, and as soon as circumstances would allow, sweet potatoes, yams, cassava, rice, beans, peas, plantains, oranges, and all sorts of fruit trees were planted in succession. In the month of October, 1837, I again set off for Haïti, in a coppered brig of 150 tons, bought for the purpose, and in five days and a half, from St. Mary's in Georgia, landed my son's wife and children at Porte Plate, together with the wives and children of his servants, now working for him under an indenture of nine years; also two additional families of my slaves, all liberated for the express purpose of transportation to Haïti, where they were all to have as much good land in fee, as they could cultivate, say ten acres for each family, and all its proceeds, together with one-fourth part of the net proceeds of their labor from my son's farm, for themselves; also victuals, clothes, medical attendance, &c., gratis, besides Saturdays and Sundays, as days of labor for themselves, or for rest, just at their option.[24]

On my arrival at my son's place, called Cabaret (twenty-seven miles east of Porte Plate) in November, 1837, as before stated, I found everything in the most flattering and prosperous condition. They had all enjoyed good health, were overflowing with the most delicious variety and abundance of fruits and provisions, and were overjoyed at again meeting their wives and children, whom they could introduce into good comfortable log houses all nicely white-washed, and in the midst of a profuse abundance of good provisions, as they had generally cleared five or six acres of land each, which being very rich, and planted with every variety to eat or to sell, they had become traders in rice, corn, potatoes, sugar cane, fowls, peas, beans, in short every thing to sell on their own account, and had already laid up thirty or forty dollars apiece. My son's farm was upon a larger scale, and furnished with more commodious dwelling houses, also with store and out houses. In nine months he had made and housed three crops of corn of twenty-five bushels to the acre, each, or one crop every three months. His high land rice, which was equal to any in Carolina, so ripe and heavy as some of it to be couched or leaned down, and no bird had ever troubled it, nor had any of the fields ever been hoed,[25] there being as yet no appearance of grass. His cotton was of an excellent staple; in seven months it had attained the height of fifteen feet;[26] the stalks were ten inches in circumference, and had up-

24. Kingsley characterized his son's policies as generous on his part, but they were prescribed by the *Rural Code*. "Cultivators" were entitled to one-fourth of all they raise, the entire produce of "their own private gardens, cultivated by themselves during their hours or days of rest," and "the necessary medicines." "The labors of the field shall commence on Monday morning, not to cease until Friday evening." *The Rural Code of Haiti,* 11, 14, 30.

25. The original newspaper version of the letter included the phrase "or required hoing," here.

26. The original newspaper version of the letter had "thirteen feet" instead of "fifteen feet" here.

wards of five hundred large boles on each stalk, (not a worm or red bug as yet to be seen.) His yams, cassava, and sweet potatoes, were incredibly large, and plentifully thick in the ground; one kind of sweet potato, lately introduced from Taheite (formerly Otaheite) Island in the Pacific, was of peculiar excellence; it tasted like new flour, and grew to an ordinary size in one month. Those I ate at my son's had been planted five weeks, and were as big as our full-grown Florida potatoes. His sweet orange-trees budded upon wild stalks cut off, (which every where abound) about six months before, had large tops, and the buds were swelling as if preparing to flower. My son reported that his people had all enjoyed excellent health, and had labored just as steadily as they formerly did in Florida, and were well satis-fied with their situation, and the advantageous exchange of circumstances they had made. They all enjoyed the friendship of the neighboring inhabit-ants, and the entire confidence of the Haïtien government.

I remained with my son all January, 1838, and assisted him in making improvements of different kinds, amongst which was a new two story house, and then left him to go to Port-au-Prince, where I obtained a favourable answer from the President of Haïti, to his petition, asking for leave to own in fee simple, the same tract of land upon which he then lived as a tenant, paying rent to the Haïtien Government, which was ordered to be surveyed to him, and valued, and not expected to exceed the sum of three thousand dollars.[27] After obtaining this land in fee for my son, I returned to Florida in February, 1838.

As France has now consented to the independence of Haïti, to which it has formally relinquished all its claims,[28] I will say a few words, in answer to some objections which I have heard made by very prudent people, to the policy of encouraging the growth and civilization of the Island of Haïti, which objections I presume, originated in the fear of having a free colored Government and powerful people, so near our own slaveholding States. If this evil of situation, arising from a natural cause, could be obviated, it certainly would be prudent to remove it. But as Haïti enjoys so many perma-nent natural advantages over any equal portion of our neighboring conti-nent, either as it relates to climate, soil, or situation, moreover its great extent and extraordinary fertility render it capable of supporting a popula-

27. This sentence read differently in the original newspaper version of the letter: "asking for leave to hold and own in fee simple, the same tract of land upon which he then lived as a tenant, paying rent to the Haïtien Government, containing about thirty-five thousand acres, which was ordered to be surveyed to him, and valued, and not expected to exceed the sum of three thousand dollars, or about ten cents an acre."
28. France recognized the independence of Haiti in 1825.

tion, of at least fourteen millions of people, which, independent of all our efforts to the contrary, will fill up by natural increase in a few years, would it not be our best policy to cultivate a friendly understanding with a formidable people, improve their moral habits, and advance their civilization as fast as lies in our power? Haïti was formerly the commercial emporium of the western world; it supplied both hemispheres with sugar and coffee; it is now recovering fast from a state of anarchy and destitution, brought on by the French Revolution. Its Government stands on a very respectable footing, and it only requires capital and education, to become a country of great commercial importance, and able to supply the whole consumption of the United States with sugar and coffee. The European nations are now taking advantage of this state of things, and are cultivating a friendly commercial intercourse with Haïti. Is it not our best policy to profit by the natural advantages which we have over them, arising from circumstances peculiar to our situation, and encourage as fast as possible the industrious and most respectable part of our free colored population, especially the agricultural part, to emigrate to that country, now mostly vacant, which is within a week's sail of our own coast? The natural attachment of those emigrants toward the country of their birth would greatly help to promote harmony and good will by an assimilation of manners, customs, and language, tending to strengthen the chain of commercial relations much to our advantage.[29]

Finally, sir, I have to observe, that if any colored people of the above description should apply to you for further information regarding Haïti, you may assure them of a good reception at George Kingsley's establishment near Porte Plate, where they will find plenty of good land to cultivate, which they may either rent or buy upon the most liberal terms; and that six months' labor as agriculturalists, will render them entirely independent of all future want of provision.[30] You may also assure them of Haïti's being comparatively a much healthier country than any of our seaboard countries south of New-York.

I remain, very respectfully, your most obedient,

z. KINGSLEY, *A Florida Planter.*

29. This sentence read differently in the original newspaper version of the letter: "The natural attachment of those emigrants towards the country of their birth would greatly tend to promote a reciprocal national attachment, and would produce harmony and good will by an assimilation of manners, customs, and language, tending to strengthen the chain of commercial relations much to our advantage."

30. Some six thousand free blacks from North America eventually responded to Boyer's call for settlers. Puig Ortiz, *Emigracion de Libertos Norteamericanos,* 7.

L. Maria Child, Letter from New York (1842)[1]

LETTER XXIII.

July 7, 1842.

It has been my fortune, in the course of a changing life, to meet with many strange characters; but I never, till lately, met with one altogether unaccountable.

Some six or eight years ago, I read a very odd pamphlet, called "The Patriarchal System of Society, as it exists under the name of Slavery; with its necessity and advantages. By an inhabitant of Florida." The writer assumes that "the patriarchal system constitutes the bond of social compact; and is better adapted for strength, durability, and independence, than any state of society hitherto adopted."

"The prosperous state of our northern neighbors," says he, "proceeds, in many instances, indirectly from southern slave labour; though they are not aware of it." This was written in 1829; read in these days of universal southern bankruptcy, it seems ludicrous; as if it had been intended for sarcasm, rather than sober earnest.

But the main object of this singular production is to prove that *colour* ought not to be the badge of degradation; that the only distinction should be

---

1. Printed Letter. Lydia Maria Child (1802–80) was a prominent abolitionist and the coeditor with her husband David Lee Child of the *National Anti-Slavery Standard* (New York). They edited the weekly newspaper from 1841 to 1843. Most of this letter first appeared as "Letters from New York.—No. 30" in the July 7, 1842, issue of the *National Anti-Slavery Standard*. The version presented here is "Letter XXIII" in L. Maria Child, *Letters from New-York* (New York: Charles S. Francis, 1843), 141–50. For an annotated edition of this book, see Lydia Maria Child, *Letters from New-York,* ed. Bruce Mills (Athens: University of Georgia Press, 1998). On Child, see Clifford, *Crusader for Freedom;* Carolyn L. Karcher, *The First Woman of the Republic: A Cultural Biography of Lydia Maria Child* (Durham: Duke University Press, 1994).

between *slave* and *free*—not between *white* and *coloured*. That the free people of colour, instead of being persecuted, and driven from the Southern States, ought to be made eligible to all offices and means of wealth. This would form, he thinks, a grand chain of security, by which the interests of the two castes would become united, and the slaves be kept in permanent subordination. Intermarriage between the races he strongly advocates; not only as strengthening the bond of union between castes that otherwise naturally war upon each other, but as a great improvement of the human race. "The intermediate grades of colour," says he, "are not only healthy, but, when condition is favourable, they are improved in shape, strength, and beauty. Daily experience shows that there is no natural antipathy between the castes on account of colour. It only requires to repeal laws as impolitic as they are unjust and unnatural—laws which confound beauty, merit, and condition, in one state of infamy and degradation on account of complexion. It is only required to leave nature to find out a safe and wholesome remedy for evils, which of all others are the most deplorable, because they are morally irreconcilable with the fundamental principles of happiness and self-preservation."[2]

I afterwards heard that Z. Kinsley, the author of this pamphlet, lived with a coloured wife, and treated her and her children with kindness and consideration. A traveller, writing from Florida, stated that he visited a planter, whose coloured wife sat at the head of the table, surrounded by healthy and handsome children. That the parlour was full of portraits of African beauties, to which the gentleman drew his attention, with much exultation; dwelling with great earnestness on the superior physical endowments of the coloured race, and the obvious advantages of amalgamation. I at once conjectured that this eccentric planter was the author of the pamphlet on the patriarchal system.

Soon after, it was rumoured that Mr. Kinsley had purchased a large tract of land of the Haitien government; that he had carried his slaves there, and given them lots. Then I heard that it was a colony, established for the advantage of his own mulatto sons; that the workmen were in a qualified kind of slavery, by consent of the government; and that he still held a large number of slaves in Florida.

Last week, this individual, who had so much excited my curiosity, was in the city; and I sought an interview. I found his conversation entertaining,

2. Kingsley revised the passage that Child quoted here in the third and fourth editions of his *Treatise*, removing references to the improved "shape, strength and beauty" of the "intermediate grades of color."

but marked by the same incongruity, that characterizes his writings and his practice. His head is a peculiar one; it would, I think, prove as great a puzzle to phrenologists, as he himself is to moralists and philosophers.

I told him of the traveller's letter, and asked if he were the gentleman described.

"I never saw the letter;" he replied; "but from what you say, I have no doubt that I am the man. I always thought and said, that the coloured race were superior to us, physically and morally. They are more healthy, have more graceful forms, softer skins,[3] and sweeter voices. They are more docile and affectionate, more faithful in their attachments, and less prone to mischief, than the white race. If it were not so, they could not have been kept in slavery."

"It is a shameful and a shocking thought," said I, "that we should keep them in slavery by reason of their very virtues."

"It is so, ma'am; but, like many other shameful things, it is true."

"Where did you obtain your portraits of coloured beauties?"

"In various places. Some of them I got on the coast of Africa. If you want to see beautiful specimens of the human race, you should see some of the native women there."

"Then you have been on the coast of Africa?"

"Yes, ma'am; I carried on the slave trade several years."

"You announce that fact very coolly," said I. "Do you you [sic] know that, in New England, men look upon a slave-trader with as much horror as they do upon a pirate?"

"Yes; and I am glad of it. They will look upon a slaveholder just so, by and by. Slave trading was very respectable business when I was young. The first merchants in England and America were engaged in it. Some people hide things which they think other people don't like. I never conceal anything."

"Where did you become acquainted with your wife?"

"On the coast of Africa, ma'am. She was a new nigger, when I first saw her."

"What led you to become attached to her?"

"She was a fine, tall figure, black as jet, but very handsome. She was very capable, and could carry on all the affairs of the plantation in my absence, as well as I could myself. She was affectionate and faithful, and I could trust her. I have fixed her nicely in my Haitien colony. I wish you would go there. She would give you the best in the house. You *ought* to go, to see how happy

3. The words *softer skins* were not in the *National Anti-Slavery Standard* version.

the human race can be. It is in a fine, rich valley, about thirty miles from Port Platte; heavily timbered with mahogany all round; well watered; flowers so beautiful: fruits in abundance, so delicious that you could not refrain from stopping to eat, till you could eat no more. My son has laid out good roads, and built bridges and mills; the people are improving, and everything is prosperous. I am anxious to establish a good school there. I engaged a teacher; but somebody persuaded him it was mean to teach niggers, and so he fell off from his bargain."

"I have heard that you hold your labourers in a sort of qualified slavery; and some friends of the coloured race have apprehensions that you may sell them again."

"My labourers in Haiti are not slaves.[4] They are a kind of indented apprentices. I give them land, and they bind themselves to work for me. I have no power to take them away from that island; and you know very well that I could not sell them there."

"I am glad you have relinquished the power to make slaves of them again. I had charge of a fine, intelligent fugitive, about a year ago. I wanted to send him to your colony; but I did not dare to trust you."

"You need not have been afraid, ma'am. I should be the last man on earth to give up a runaway. If my own were to run away, I wouldn't go after 'em."[5]

"If these are your feelings, why don't you take *all* your slaves to Haiti?"

"I have thought that subject all over, ma'am; and I have settled it in my own mind. All we can do in this world is to balance evils. I want to do great things for Haiti; and in order to do them, I must have money. If I have no negroes to cultivate my Florida lands, they will run to waste; and then I can raise no money from them for the benefit of Haiti. I do all I can to make them comfortable, and they love me like a father. They would do any thing on earth to please me. Once I stayed away longer than usual, and they thought I was dead. When I reached home, they overwhelmed me with their caresses; I could hardly stand it."

"Does it not grieve you to think of leaving these faithful, kind-hearted people to the cruel chances of slavery?"

"Yes, it does; but I hope to get all my plans settled in a few years."

---

4. Haitian "cultivators" had to enter into a contract or "reciprocal engagement" with a proprietor for a term of from two to nine years. *The Rural Code of Haiti*, 10.

5. In the *National Anti-Slavery Standard* letter, Child included "I think" at the end of this quotation from Kingsley.

"You tell me you are seventy-six years old; what if you should die before your plans are completed?"

"Likely enough I shall. In that case, my heirs would break my will, I dare say, and my poor niggers would be badly off."

"Then manumit them now; and avoid this dreadful risk."

"I have thought that all over, ma'am; and I have settled it that I can do more good by keeping them in slavery a few years more. The best we can do in this world is to balance evils judiciously."[6]

"But you do not balance wisely. Remember that all the descendants of your slaves, through all coming time, will be affected by your decision."

"So will all in Haiti be affected, through all coming time, if I can carry out my plans. To do good in the world, we *must* have money. That's the way I reasoned when I carried on the slave trade. It was very profitable then."

"And do you have no remorse of conscience, in recollecting that bad business?"

"*Some* things I do not like to remember; but they were not things in which I was to blame; they were inevitably attendant on the trade."

I argued that any trade must be wicked, that *had* such inevitable consequences. He admitted it; but still clung to his balance of evils. If that theory is admitted in morals at all, I confess that his practice seems to me a legitimate, though an extreme result. But it was altogether vain to argue with him about fixed principles of right and wrong; one might as well fire small shot at the hide of a rhinoceros. Yet were there admirable points about him;—perseverance, that would conquer the world; an heroic candour, that avowed all things, creditable and discreditable; and kindly sympathies, too—though it must be confessed that they go groping and floundering about in the strangest fashion.

He came from Scotland; no other country, perhaps, except New-England, could have produced such a character. His father was a Quaker; and he still loves to attend Quaker meetings; particularly silent ones, where he says he has planned some of his best bargains.[7] To complete the circle of

6. Kingsley's argument here is remarkably similar to William Harper's in Harper's *Memoir on Slavery*: "the condition of our whole existence is but to struggle with evils—to compare them—to choose between them, and so far as we can, to mitigate them. To say that there is evil in any institution, is only to say that it is human." William Harper, *Memoir on Slavery, Read before the Society for the Advancement of Learning at its Annual Meeting in Columbia, 1837* (Charleston, S.C.: James S. Burges, 1838), 8.

7. The *National Anti-Slavery Standard* letter does not include the phrase "where he says he has planned some of his best bargains."

contradictions, he likes the abolitionists, and is a prodigious admirer of George Thompson.[8]

"My neighbours call me an abolitionist," said he; "I tell them that they may do so, in welcome; for it is a pity they shouldn't have *one* case of amalgamation to point at."

This singular individual has been conversant with all sorts of people, and seen almost all parts of the world. "I have known the Malay and the African, the North American Indian, and the European," said he; "and the more I've seen of the world, the less I understand it. It's a queer place; that's a fact."

Probably this mixture with people of all creeds and customs, combined with the habit of looking *outward* for his guide of action, may have bewildered his moral sense, and produced his system of "balancing evils!" A theory obviously absurd, as well as slippery in its application; for none but God *can* balance evils; it requires omniscience and omnipresence to do it.

His conversation produced great activity of thought on the subject of conscience, and of that "light that lighteth every man who cometh into the world."[9] Whether this utilitarian remembers it or not, he must have stifled many convictions before he arrived at his present state of mind. And so it must have been with "the pious John Newton," whose devotional letters from the coast of Africa, while he was slave-trading there, record "sweet

8. George Thompson (1804–78) was a prominent, militant British abolitionist. An excellent orator, Thompson first arrived in the United States in September 1834, at the invitation of William Lloyd Garrison. Thompson was particularly popular with women's antislavery societies, but throughout the northern states he more frequently met with the violence of antiabolitionist mobs. After a visit to New York in May 1835, Thompson spent most of the rest of his time in Boston. In November, he was smuggled out of that city and placed on board a boat for Halifax. President Andrew Jackson, in a message to Congress in December 1835, denounced Thompson as a meddling foreign emissary. Thompson returned to England in 1836, where he continued to support Garrison and the radical abolitionists. After traveling to India in 1843, Thompson returned to England where he served as a member of Parliament from 1847 to 1852. Ironically, when Thompson returned for a third visit to the United States in 1864, he was honored with invitations from both Congress and President Lincoln. In 1865 he accompanied Garrison and Major Robert Anderson aboard the ship that returned the American flag to Fort Sumter in the harbor of Charleston, South Carolina. Betty Fladeland, *Men and Brothers: Anglo-American Antislavery Cooperation* (Urbana: University of Illinois Press, 1972), 197–98, 225–29, 368, 410; Howard Temperley, *British Antislavery, 1833–1870* (London: Longman, 1972), 22–29, 237–39, 256; C. Duncan Rice, "The Anti-Slavery Mission of George Thompson to the United States, 1834–1835," *Journal of American Studies* 2 (1968): 13–31.

9. The biblical reference is to John 1:9: "That was the true Light, which lighteth every man that cometh into the world."

seasons of communion with his God."[10] That *he* was not left without a witness within him, is proved by the fact, that in his journal he expresses gratitude to God for opening the door for him to leave the slave trade, by providing other employment. The monitor *within* did not deceive him; but his education was at war with its dictates, because it taught him that whatever was *legalized* was *right*. Plain as the guilt of the slave trade now is, to every man, woman, and child, it was not so in the time of Clarkson; had it been otherwise, there would have been no need of his labours.[11] He was accused of planning treason and insurrection, plots were laid against his life, and the difficulty of combating his obviously just principles, led to the vilest misrepresentations and the most false assumptions.[12] Thus it must always be with those who attack a very corrupt public opinion.

The slave *trade,* which all civilized laws now denounce as piracy, was defended in precisely the same spirit that *slavery* is now. Witness the following remarks from Boswell, the biographer of Dr. Johnson, whose opinions echo the tone of genteel society:[13]

"I beg leave to enter my most solemn protest against Dr. Johnson's general doctrine with respect to the slave trade. I will resolutely say that his unfavourable notion of it was owing to prejudice, and imperfect or false information. The *wild* and *dangerous* attempt which has

10. John Newton (1725–1807) spent much of his youth at sea. Converted to Christianity as a young man, Newton also became a slave trader. Ill health forced him to take a position in the Customs House, where he came under the influence of revivalists George Whitefield and John Wesley. In 1764, after being ordained into the Christian ministry, he became curate of Olney, Buckinghamshire, England. When William Cowper settled in the area, the two men jointly published the *Olney Hymns.* Newton's writings proved influential both in religious matters and in the opposition to the slave trade. Bernard Martin, *John Newton: A Biography* (London: William Heinemann, 1950).

11. Thomas Clarkson (1760–1846) was an English abolitionist, who gathered information on the slave trade to influence Parliament. Together with William Wilberforce, Clarkson was primarily responsible for the 1807 act abolishing the British slave trade. Ellen Gibson Wilson, *Thomas Clarkson: A Biography* (London: Macmillan, 1989).

12. In the *National Anti-Slavery Standard* version of this letter, this sentence was two sentences that read "He was accused of plotting treason and insurrection, with as much bitterness as abolitionists now are. Plots were laid against his life; and the difficulty of combating his obviously just principles, led to the same misrepresentations and false assumptions which we now have to encounter."

13. James Boswell (1740–95) was a Scottish author. His *The Life of Samuel Johnson, LL.D.* earned him distinction as one of the greatest biographers in Western literature. Boswell also kept voluminous journals in which he recorded Johnson's daily life in detail. Dr. Samuel Johnson (1709–84) was a prominent English author and literary critic, whose publications won him wide acclaim in eighteenth-century England.

for some time been persisted in, to obtain an act of our legislature to abolish so very *important and necessary a branch of commercial interest,* must have been crushed at once, had not the *insignificance* of the zealots, who vainly took the lead in it, made the vast body of planters, merchants, and others, whose immense properties are involved in that trade, reasonably enough suppose that there could be no danger. The encouragement which the attempt has received, excites my wonder and indignation; and though some men of superior abilities have supported it, (whether from a love of temporary popularity when prosperous, or a love of general mischief when desperate,) my opinion is unshaken. To abolish a status which in all ages *God has sanctioned,* and man continued, would not only be robbery to an innumerable class of our fellow subjects, but it would be extreme cruelty to African savages; a portion of whom it saves from massacre, or intolerable bondage in their own country, and introduces into a much happier state of life; especially now, when their passage to the West Indies, and their treatment there, is humanely regulated. *To abolish that trade, would be to shut the gates of mercy on mankind.*"[14]

These changes in the code of morals adopted by society, by no means unsettle my belief in eternal and unchangeable principles of right and wrong; neither do they lead me to doubt that in all these cases men inwardly know better than they act. The slaveholder, when he manumits on his deathbed, thereby acknowledges that he has known he was doing wrong. Public opinion expresses what men *will* to do; not their inward *perceptions.* All kinds of crimes have been countenanced by public opinion, in some age or nation; but we cannot as easily show how far they were sustained by reason and conscience in each individual. I believe the lamp never goes out, though it may shine dimly through a foggy atmosphere.

This consideration should renew our zeal to purify public opinion; to let no act or word of ours help to corrupt it, in the slightest degree. How shall we fulfil this sacred trust, which each holds for the good of all? Not by calculating consequences; not by balancing evils; but by reverent obedience to our own highest convictions of individual duty.[15]

14. Child italicized the words in this long quotation from Boswell's *Life of Johnson* to emphasize what she considered to be the scandalous nature of Boswell's defense of the slave trade. Child's punctuation and capitalization vary slightly from Boswell's. George Birkbeck Hill, ed., *Boswell's Life of Johnson* (New York: Harper and Brothers, 1891), 3:231–32.

15. The version of the letter that appeared in the *National Anti-Slavery Standard* ended here. Child added the final five paragraphs when she assembled her letters for publication in 1843.

Few men ask concerning right and wrong of their own hearts. Few listen to the oracle *within*, which can only be heard in the stillness. The merchant seeks his moral standard on 'Change—a fitting name for a thing so fluctuating; the sectary in the opinion of his small theological department; the politician in the tumultuous echo of his party; the worldling in the buzz of saloons. In a word, each man inquires of *his* public; what wonder, then, that the answers are selfish as trading interest, blind as local prejudice, and various as human whim?

A German drawing-master once told me of a lad who wished to sketch landscapes from nature. The teacher told him that the first object was to choose some *fixed point of view*. The sagacious pupil chose a cow grazing beneath the trees. Of course, his *fixed point* soon began to move hither and thither, as she was attracted by the sweetness of the pasturage; and the lines of his drawing fell into strange confusion.

This a correct type of those who choose public opinion for their moral fixed point of view. It moves according to the provender before it, and they who trust to it have but a whirling and distorted landscape.

Coleridge defines public opinion as "the average prejudices of the community."[16] Wo unto those who have no safer guide of principle and practice than this "average of prejudices." Wo unto them in an especial manner, in these latter days, when "The windows of heaven are opened, and *therefore* the foundations of the earth do *shake!*"[17]

Feeble wanderers are they, following a flickering Jack-o'lantern, when there is a calm, bright pole-star for ever above the horizon, to guide their steps, if they would but look to it.

16. Samuel Taylor Coleridge (1772–1834) was an English Romantic poet.

17. The biblical reference is to Isaiah 24:18: "And it shall come to pass, that he who fleeth from the noise of the fear shall fall into the pit; and he that cometh up out of the midst of the pit shall be taken in the snare: for the windows from on high are open, and the foundations of the earth do shake."

Last Will and Testament (1843)[1]

I, Zephaniah Kingsley, of Duval County, Florida, Planter, being of sound mind, memory and understanding, do make and publish this my last Will and Testament, as follows, viz:

First. I will and devise that all my just and lawful, funeral and testamentary charges, and expenses shall be fully paid and discharged, as soon as may be after my death.

Secondly. To my nephew Kingsley B. Gibbs[2] I will and devise one half of my two thousand acre Tract of Land in the Twelve Mile Swamp which when divided into two parts will give one thousand acres of land for his one half be the same more or less, to him, his heirs or assigns: I also bequeath to him in fee, my schooner North Carolina with all its appurtenances, likewise any books and arms not otherwise disposed of.

Third. To my nephew George Couper Gibbs[3] I will and bequeath in fee

1. Typed Transcript. Case file for *Kingsley et al. v. Broward et al.*, 19 Florida 722 (1883), Florida State Archives, Tallahassee, Fla. Someone removed the original will from Kingsley's Duval County probate file. Probate Record for Zephaniah Kingsley (1843), #1203, Probate Department, Duval County Courthouse, Jacksonville, Fla.

2. Kingsley Beatty Gibbs (1810–59) was the son of Zephaniah Kingsley's sister Isabella and George Gibbs. Born in New York, Kingsley Beatty Gibbs and his family moved to Florida shortly after it became an American territory in 1821. The young Gibbs was a court official, a militia officer, and a member of the territorial legislature. In March 1839, Gibbs purchased the Fort George Island plantation from his uncle Zephaniah Kingsley, and two years later, he settled into the life of a planter. Gibbs owned the plantation until 1853. Jacqueline C. Fretwell, *Kingsley Beatty Gibbs and His Journal of 1840–1843* (St. Augustine, Fla.: St. Augustine Historical Society, 1984), 3–5, 11; Stowell, *Timucuan Ecological and Historic Preserve*, 46–54.

3. George Couper Gibbs (1822–73) was the son of Zephaniah Kingsley's sister Isabella and George Gibbs and a younger brother of Kingsley Beatty Gibbs. Born in Georgia, he served in the army during the Mexican War. Settling in Florida in 1850, he operated a sawmill at the mouth of the St. Johns River. During the Civil War, he served as a colonel in the Confederate Army. Margaret Gibbs Watt, *The Gibbs Family of Long Ago and Near at Hand, 1337–1967* (privately printed, n.d.), 21–22.

simple, absolute, all the remaining one half of the aforementioned two thousand acre tract in Twelve Mile Swamp, which will be one thousand acres be the same more or less.

Fourthly. To my nephew Charles J. McNeil I will and bequeath in fee simple, absolute, a certain tract or parcel of land situate on Beauclerc's Bluff, between Cohen & Curry, containing Sixty two and one half acres of Land be the same more or less; also my three hundred acre tract situate at the head of six mile creek (Saw Mill Creek) flat. Also my negro woman Betsy and Peggy the daughter of Nancy and all their children and issue; Also, one of my horses saddle &c. at his choice, all the above to him in fee & to his heirs &c.

Fifth. To George Kingsley[4] my son by Anna Madegigine Jai Kingsley I will and bequeath all my nautical instruments including maps, charts &c. to be sent out to him at Hayti by way of New York or otherwise, clear of expense to him.

Sixth. It is my will and desire, that as soon after my decease as is convenient to my Executors, that all the specific legacies and devises aforesaid shall be separated, set apart and reversed, by my Executors for the special purposes aforesaid and that all the remaining part of my property, real and personal, including what sums may be received from Government in compensation of losses in 1812 or 13, or since of what nature or kind soever after the payment of my just debts,[5] shall by my Executors, or their assigns, be sold or converted into money, and the net amount be divided in twelve equal parts or shares (12 parts) or shares,[6] one of which parts shall be paid to my nephew Kingsley B. Gibbs in full compensation for all claim that he may have or devise against my Estate.[7] One part (say 1/12th) shall be paid to Anna Madegigine Jai Kingsley or to her heirs or assigns.[8] Two parts (2)

4. See n. 4 on p. 24.
5. The heirs of John Fraser, for whose estate Zephaniah Kingsley served as executor, made claims upon Kingsley's estate. They eventually received $15,000. Zephaniah Kingsley Probate Record.
6. The twelfth share was to be paid to Kingsley's nephew, Charles J. McNeill. His share is not mentioned in this transcription of the will, but other documents in the probate record and other court records indicate that the twelfth share, missing from this transcription, was designated for McNeill. Zephaniah Kingsley Probate Record; "Petition," July 27, 1845, Superior Court of East Florida Records, Patriot War Papers and Claims, St. Johns County Records, St. Augustine Historical Society, St. Augustine, Fla.
7. Kingsley Beatty Gibbs received at least $1,100 from his uncle Zephaniah Kingsley's estate in addition to his fees as executor. Zephaniah Kingsley Probate Record.
8. Anna M. Kingsley received at least $2,325 from her husband Zephaniah Kingsley's estate. Zephaniah Kingsley Probate Record.

to John Maxwell Kingsley, my son by Anna M. Jai.[9] Four parts (4) to be paid to George Kingsley, my son by Anna M. Jai.[10] Two parts (2) to be paid to Flora H. Kingsley[11] her heirs or assigns, One (1) part to be paid to Micanopy the son of Sarah M. Kingsley, should he live until the years of discretion.[12] All the foregoing legacies and bequests in this Will are granted in fee simple, absolute, on condition that no further claim or action at law shall be instituted or suggested by any of the parties against my Estate except the usual lawful charges and commissions.

Seventh. I do hereby declare that it is and shall be lawful, for my Executors to retain in their hands sufficient money of the proceeds of my Estate, to defray all necessary charges and expenses in the administration thereof before paying over the surplus as aforesaid.

Eighth. I do hereby order and direct, that whenever I may happen to die that my body may be buried in the nearest, most convenient place without any Religious ceremony whatever, and that it may be excused from the usual indiscreet formalities and parade of washing, dressing &c., or exposure in any way, but removed just as it died to the common burying ground.[13]

Ninth. Should I leave any Slaves, I earnestly recommend to my Executors

9. John Maxwell Kingsley received at least $3,000 from his father Zephaniah Kingsley's estate. Zephaniah Kingsley Probate Record.

10. George Kingsley's estate received at least $6,000 from Zephaniah Kingsley's estate. Zephaniah Kingsley Probate Record.

11. Flora Hanahan Kingsley (d. 1875), was one of Kingsley's slaves, whom he freed with her mother in 1828. Zephaniah and Flora Kingsley had at least four sons—Charles (c. 1829–52), James, William, and Osceola. She emigrated with her children to Haiti in 1842. She eventually received nearly $4,500 from Zephaniah Kingsley's estate. Zephaniah Kingsley Probate Record.

After her death, her three surviving sons tried unsuccessfully to establish their claim to some 300 acres of land deeded by Zephaniah Kingsley to Flora, Charles, James, and "other natural or legitimate children or child, which may be born of her body during her life, and of quarteroon breed; or such children as the aforesaid Flora shall acknowledge to have been produced by sexual intercourse with a white man, to them and their heirs and assigns forever." *Kingsley et al. v. Broward et al.* 19 Florida 722–47 (1883); Schafer, "A Class of People Neither Freemen Nor Slaves," 605, n. 30.

12. Micanopy Kingsley received at least $1,100 from Zephaniah Kingsley's estate. Zephaniah Kingsley Probate Record.

13. Apparently, New York officials were ignorant of or disregarded Kingsley's wishes. An undertaker took his body and buried it in a Quaker cemetery in the city of New York. May, "Zephaniah Kingsley, Nonconformist," 156–57.

not to separate the families by selling them individually without their consent, if to be avoided.[14]

Tenth. It is my will and I do hereby authorize my Executors not to separate the families but to allow to any of my slaves the privilege of purchasing their freedom at one half the price of their valuation, on consideration of

14. On March 13, 1844, appraisers prepared an inventory of Kingsley's personal property and assigned values to each item. His personal property was worth $32,080, of which nearly $30,000 was property in slaves. The inventory included the following list of slaves, arranged in family groups:

Man	Woman	Children	Value
José	Penda	Mira, Nacebo, Mary, William	$1,998
Carpenter Bill	Hannah	Frank, Lavinia, Alonzo, Marianne, Bill	$3,605
Carpenter Bonify	Mary	Beck, Scipio, Louis, Esther, George, Tena, June, Sarah	$4,620
Lindo	Sophey	Labo, George, Philip	$1,800
Jenoma	Jenny	Mike, Augustus	$1,100
	Betty	Patty, Jenny	$849
	Qualla	Letitia, Victorine	$636
Horse Bill	Yamba	Bolivar	$750
Abdalla	Bella	Paul, Amie	$1,248
Tamba	Conta	Monroe, Jeffrey, Thomas	$1,425
Prince	Julia		$1,100
Sam	Elsey		$1,100
Jim	Becca		$1,100
Hannibal	Peggy	Eliza, Nancy	$1,500
Andrew	Nanny	Jacob, Silvia,* (Adam)	$1,500
	Tamasa	Rose, Jack, David	$948
Brutus	Nancy	Chloe, Joe	$1,100
Toby	Patty		$200
C. Dick	Comba		$300
Romeo			$650
David			$550
Dick			$650
	Betsy	Celeste, John, Emma	$1,100
	Old Rose		$150
		Total worth	$29,979

In September 1846, Judge William F. Crabtree ordered Kingsley's executors to sell twenty-one of Kingsley's slaves on January 1, 1847. One of those listed died before the sale, but two others were included. Of the five family groups in this portion of Kingsley's slaves, four were sold as families. Three different slave owners divided the four members of the other family. Zephaniah Kingsley Probate Record.

For the treatment of slave "property" in wills, see Thomas D. Morris, Southern Slavery and the Law, 1619–1860 (Chapel Hill: University of North Carolina Press, 1996), 81–101; and Joan E. Cashin, "According to His Wish and Desire: Female Kin and Female Slaves in Planter Wills," in Christie Anne Farnham, ed., Women of the American South: A Multicultural Reader (New York: New York University Press, 1996), 90–119.

their migrating to Hayti, if they cannot be allowed to stay as free in this Territory.

Eleventh. I do hereby appoint Kingsley B. Gibbs, George Kingsley and Benjamin A. Putnam[15] Guardians to my infant natural children, amongst which I acknowledge all those of Flora H. Kingsley of Camp New Hope, also Sarah Murphy's mulatto child Micanopy now in Hayti: I do also solemnly enjoin my colored and natural children, that seeing the illiberal and inequitable laws of this Territory will not afford to them and to their children that protection and justice, which is due in civilized society to every human being: Always to keep by them a *Will*, ready made, and legally executed, directing the disposal of their property, after their death until they can remove themselves and properties to some land of liberty and equal rights, where the conditions of society are governed by some law less absurd than that of color. This I strongly recommend, nor do I know in what light the law may consider my acknowledged wife, Anna Madegigine Jai, as our connubial relations took place in a foreign land, where our marriage was celebrated and solemnized by her native African customs altho' never celebrated according to the forms of Christian usage; yet she has always been respected as my wife and as such I acknowledge her, nor do I think that her truth, honor, integrity, moral conduct or good sense will lose in comparison with any one.

Thirteenth. Lastly, I do hereby nominate and appoint Kingsley B. Gibbs and Benjamin A. Putnam of Florida and George Kingsley, the son of my wife, Anna Madegigine Jai, to be Executors of this my last Will and Testament, to whom I earnestly recommend the closing of the concerns of my estate &c. as expeditiously as possible, and to see that my intentions in regard to the disposition of my estate are, and shall be strictly complied with, for the better promotion of which purpose I do appoint my trusty friend Benjamin A. Putnam to act as legal attorney and advisor in all matters and things relating to the interest of my estate, with a fee to be paid to him by it of One Thousand Dollars; and I do hereby revoke all other wills by me heretofore made.

In Witness I, the said Zephaniah Kingsley, the testator, have to this my last Will and Testament contained in this sheet of paper set my hand and seal

15. Benjamin A. Putnam (b. c. 1802) was a native of Georgia. In 1850, he was the Surveyor General for the State of Florida and owned real property worth $3,500 and fourteen slaves. His household included his wife, Hellen, a native of Connecticut, and their eighteen-year-old daughter. Duval County, Florida, Seventh Census of the United States, 1850.

this twentieth day of July in the year One Thousand Eight Hundred and forty three (July 1843).

ZEPHn KINGSLEY (SEAL)

Signed, sealed, published and declared by the said Zephaniah Kingsley as and for his last Will and Testament in the presence of us who have at his request hereunto subscribed our names as witnesses thereto in the presence of the said testator and of each other at Jacksonville 20 July 1843.

THOMAS O. HOLMES[16]

WILLIAM S. DONALDSON[17]

DAVID MCCUEN[18]

16. Thomas O. Holmes (b. c. 1820) was a native of Maine. In 1850, he was a merchant in Duval County and owned real property worth $5,000 and seven slaves. Duval County, Florida, Seventh Census of the United States, 1850.

17. William S. Donaldson (b. c. 1805) was a native of Massachusetts. In 1850 he was a carpenter in Duval County and owned real property worth $1,500 and one female slave. His household included his wife, Emilla, a native of Florida, their three children, as well as black-smith William Ward, his wife, and an older woman. Duval County, Florida, Seventh Census of the United States, 1850.

18. David McCuen (b. c. 1820) was a native of Ireland. In 1850 he was a bookkeeper and owned real property worth $700 and one female slave. His household included his wife, Lucy, a native of South Carolina, and their four-year-old daughter, as well as a free black woman, Sarah Thomas, and her three-year-old daughter. Duval County, Florida, Seventh Census of the United States, 1850.

INDEX

abolitionists, 17–18, 20–21, 48n, 55n, 112–14
"Address to the Legislative Council," 6–8, 26–35
Africa. *See* colonization, in Africa
African Americans. *See* free blacks; mulattos; quadroons/quarteroons; slaves
African Colonization Society. *See* American Colonization Society
American Colonization Society, 16, 55n, 73n, 102
American Revolution, 2, 32
Anderson, Robert, 112n

Bahia, 45n
Banda Oriental, 44n, 56n
Barbados, 9, 28, 46n, 67
Baxter, Oran, 24n
Beckles, John, 9
Berlin, Ira, 8
Bonaparte, Napoleon, 13, 48n, 50n
Boswell, James, 113–14
Boyer, Jean Pierre, 15, 19, 21, 74n, 86n, 96, 98
Brazil, 32, 43–45, 56, 63–64
British colonies, 9, 45, 46n, 52, 55, 67n
Bryan, James W., 52n
Buenos Aires, Republic of, 43, 44n, 56

Canada. *See* colonization, in Canada
caste. *See* class
Castillo y Lanzas, Joaquín María del, 80n
Castro y Ferrer, Bartolome de, 25

Chidgigine, Sophy, 4n
Child, David Lee, 18, 107
Child, Lydia Maria, 18, 20, 107–15
Christianity, 10, 17–18, 29, 54n, 68n, 70–71, 88–89. *See also* missionaries; preachers; Quakers
Christian Statesman, 102
Christophe, Henri, 96n
Cisplatine Province, 44n
Clarke, Charles W., 84
Clarke, George J. F., 84
Clarkson, Thomas, 113
class, 1, 17, 28–29, 44–45, 53, 60, 66, 90, 93
Cockburn, Sir George, 63n
Code Noir, 46n
Coffee, Joshua A., 85
coffee, 48–49, 64, 94, 106
Coleridge, Samuel Taylor, 115
colonization, 14–16, 18; in Africa, 19, 33–34, 54, 55n, 73–74; in Canada, 76n, 78–79; in Haiti, 15, 18–20, 23n, 34, 73n, 74, 76n, 99n, 102, 106n, 108–11, 119–20; in Mexico, 18–19, 76n, 79–81
Congress, U.S., 11–12, 82–85
Cooper, Adam, 85
cotton, 5, 37, 62, 72, 94
Cowper, William, 113n
Crabtree, William F., 119n
Cuba, 27, 46n, 55, 56n
Cumberland Island, Georgia, 63

Danaides, 57
Danaus, 57n
Demerara, 28, 67
Dessalines, Jean-Jacques, 50n, 96n
Dominican Republic. *See* Santo Domingo/
  Dominican Republic
Dom Pedro I, 56n
Donald, David, 17
Donaldson, William S., 121
Drayton, William, 16
Dutch colonies, 9, 29, 46, 47n
Duval, William P., 5, 12

East Florida Herald (St. Augustine), 36–38
emancipation, 31, 32n, 33, 44n, 54n, 55. *See
  also* manumission
Entralgo, Juan de, 25
Estrada, Juan José de, 25n, 70n
Evans, George H., 76n, 86n, 87, 91, 94,
  98

Florida, 35; as an American territory, 2, 5, 13,
  22, 82–84; climate of, 1, 13, 27–28, 37, 41,
  62; free blacks in, 28–29, 36–37, 59;
  immigration to, 22, 62; racial attitudes in,
  2, 22, 65–66, 120; as a Spanish colony, 1–2,
  5, 11–12, 22, 70n
Fort George Island, 4, 60–61, 116n
France, 48–49, 64, 105
Franklin, James, 21
Fraser, John, 4, 117n
free blacks, 10, 27–29, 35, 46–47; alliance
  between whites and, 8–9, 29–30, 32, 37,
  43, 46, 47n, 51, 65, 108; in Brazil, 32, 43–
  45, 56; definition of, 1n, 100n; legal rights
  of, 7–9, 13, 17, 33, 44–46, 47n, 52n, 54n,
  59, 63, 66, 72–73, 78, 80–81, 83; as middle
  caste, 1, 8–9, 17, 22, 28, 44–45,108; in
  militia, 29, 45, 46n, 67n
freedom of speech, 37–38
French colonies, 9, 46, 55
French Revolution, 48n, 106

Gardiner, Daniel S., 84
Garrison, William Lloyd, 76n, 112n
Genovese, Eugene, 67n, 69n
Gibbs, George, 116n
Gibbs, George Couper, 116
Gibbs, Isabella Kingsley, 116n
Gibbs, Kingsley Beatty, 116–17, 120
Gibson, Edward R., 5
Greece, 35; War of Independence in, 35n
Gullah Jack. *See* Pritchard, Jack
Gurley, Ralph Randolph, 102n

Haiti, 2, 15, 19, 35, 47, 50, 66, 73, 86–106.
  See also colonization, in Haiti; Saint
  Domingue/St. Domingo
Hanahan, Flora. *See* Kingsley, Flora Hanahan
Harper, Robert Goodloe, 14–16
Harper, William, 111n
Harvey, W. W., 21
Hernandez, Joseph Marion, 5
Holmes, Thomas O., 121

Ingenac, B., 101
Islam, 69

Jackson, Andrew, 12, 112n
Jai, Anna Madgigine. *See* Kingsley, Anna
Jamaica, 9, 46n, 67n
Jefferson, Thomas, 14–16, 22, 38
Johnson, Samuel, 113

Kindelan y Oregon, Sebastian, 25n
Kingsley, Anatoile Francois Vauntravers, 24n,
  104
Kingsley, Anna, 3, 4n, 19, 23–25, 109, 117,
  118, 120
Kingsley, Charles, 3, 118n
Kingsley, Flora Hanahan, 3, 4n, 118, 120
Kingsley, George, 3, 18–19, 20n, 23, 24n, 76n,
  117–18, 120; settlement in Haiti of, 19,
  24n, 103–6, 110
Kingsley, Isabella Johnstone, 2

Daniel W. Stowell is director and editor of the Lincoln Legal Papers, a project of the Illinois Historic Preservation Agency in Springfield, Illinois, and author of *Rebuilding Zion: The Religious Reconstruction of the South, 1863-1877* (1998).

Printed in the United States
1342000003B/318